WINNING WAYS
in HEALTH CARE

transactional analysis
for effective communication

DOROTHY JONGEWARD
Transactional Analysis
Management Institute, Inc.

MURIEL JAMES
James & James
Transactional Analysis
Institute

ADDISON-WESLEY PUBLISHING COMPANY

Reading, Massachusetts
Menlo Park, California · London · Amsterdam · Don Mills, Ontario · Sydney

Cartoons by Johnny Sajem.

Library of Congress Cataloging in Publication Data

Jongeward, Dorothy.
    Winning ways in health care.

    Bibliography: p.
    1. Medical personnel — Psychology — Problems,
exercises, etc. 2. Transactional analysis — Problems,
exercises, etc. 3. Interpersonal relations — Problems,
exercises, etc. I. James, Muriel, joint author.
II. Title.
R727.J63   158'.9   80-10896
ISBN 0-201-00451-8

INTRODUCTION

This workbook is designed as a group training tool for the rapid learning of the applications of transactional analysis to good communications in health care. The workbook can be used in conjunction with our book *Born To Win* [1]* or by itself.

Often health care training focuses on technology and skills. However, there is a growing awareness of the importance of the *human* side of health care delivery. Many people are seeing the need to deal more effectively with the "whole" person whether that person is someone with whom they work or someone they serve.

Transactional analysis, developed by Eric Berne, M.D., offers a practical approach to understanding people. Dr. Berne's theories evolved as he observed behavioral changes occurring in patients when a new stimulus, such as a word, gesture, or sound, entered their foci. These changes involved facial expressions, word intonations, sentence structure, body movements, gestures, tics, posture, and carriage. It was as though there were several people inside each individual.

---

* For a complete list of the authors' books, see Appendix A. Numbers in brackets refer to the Notes and References section, beginning on p. 139.

At times one or another of these inner people seemed to be in control of the patient's total personality. Berne observed that these various "selves" transacted with others in different ways and that these transactions could be analyzed. He saw that some of the transactions had ulterior motives and were used as a means of manipulating other people into psychological games.*

He also observed that people performed in predetermined ways, acting as if they were on stage putting on a play. This resulted in his concept of psychological scripts. Berne's observations led him to develop his unique theory called Transactional Analysis (abbreviated to TA).

Originally TA was developed as a method of psychotherapy to be used in group treatment. However, TA is not only a useful therapy tool, but also a powerful *communications tool.* It gives people a rational approach to understanding human behavior, based on the assumption that people can learn to trust themselves, make their own choices, take responsibility for their relationships, and express their feelings appropriately. Its principles are relatively easy to learn and can be applied wherever people deal with people.

One vice-president of human relations and resources who has directed a core TA training program since 1975 writes:

> At our hospital: (1) TA gives people of divergent technical backgrounds a common language. (2) TA concepts and terminology communicate clearly and save time in day-to-day, manager-to-manager situations. (3) TA makes possible a psychological context in daily managerial decision making. (4) TA provides a mirror for the individual manager while suggesting insights about others. (5) TA shorthands organization development structure and style analysis. [3]

TA is especially useful in health care because it emphasizes a caring, supportive, yet growth-oriented approach to people. It not only helps further the goal of cooperative, organic, and effective relationships among staff members, but also promotes excellence in patient care. Transactional analysis provides a tool for developing even more winning ways in health care.

NOTES TO GROUP LEADERS

We designed this workbook for group participation because we believe that group members learn much from one another. Therefore, whenever possible and practical, we suggest that you give the participants time to work together on the exercises in small groups of four to six. Much of the learning can be their responsibility. When practical, each group may give a brief summary of its experiences to the overall group.

---

* The analysis of games has received wide popularity in Berne's bestseller *Games People Play.* [2]

A few of the exercises, such as the personal questions about script, can be done individually and can be "homework" projects. However, depending on the goals and purpose of the seminar, even these may be useful to share in small groups and/or in a general class discussion. It might serve the participants to ask what they would prefer doing and to develop a contract with them around their interests.

If you use this workbook in conjunction with *Born to Win: Transactional Analysis with Gestalt Experiments*, here are our suggestions for outside reading with each unit.

Winning Ways in Health Care	Corresponding chapters in Born to Win
Unit 1	1, 4, 7
Unit 2	2, 5, 6, 9, 10
Unit 3	2
Unit 4	3
Unit 5	8
Unit 6	9
Unit 7	3, 10

A bibliography of other transactional analysis books we have written, references to other materials, and the address of the International Transactional Analysis Association (ITAA) are included in Appendix A.

The aims of our workbook are to: (1) give each participant quick insight into human relationships through the tool of transactional analysis; and (2) allow each person, through the exercises and group participation, to practice applying this tool to the people problems they may encounter in health care delivery.

We invite you to develop and to add case studies that are pertinent to the particular situation you are addressing and that illustrate the principles of good communication discussed in the text.

You have our best wishes as you work with people to increase their winning ways.

ACKNOWLEDGMENTS

We gratefully acknowledge the following persons, who have served as resources to us. They have given graciously of their ideas and feedback and have enriched this workbook.

Reverend Joe B. Abbott, M. Div.
Director, Pastoral Care and
  Counseling Services
Baptist Medical Centers
Birmingham, Alabama

Fannie Baeza, P.H.N.
Supervising Public Health Nurse
Health Care Services Agency
Alameda County, California

Barbara Biasotti, R.N., M.A.
Supervising Nurse, Intensive
   Treatment Program
California Youth Authority
Northern Reception Center-Clinic
Sacramento, California

Anita J. Brown
Director, Training and Development
Lutheran General Hospital
Park Ridge, Illinois

Claudine Leveroni, R.N.
Lecturer
Concord, California

Margaret Smith, M.S.
Psychiatric Nursing Instructor
Merritt-Hospital
Oakland, California

Jane Stein, R.N., B.S.N., M.Ed.
Instructor, Samuel Merritt Hospital
School of Nursing
Oakland, California

Patricia Anne Sullivan, R.N.
Foster McGraw Hospital
Loyola Research Medical Center
Maywood, Illinois

L. James Wylie, B.A., B.Th.
Vice President, Human Relations
   and Resources
Lutheran General Hospital
Park Ridge, Illinois

Orinda, California
Lafayette, California

May 1980

Dorothy Jongeward
Muriel James

CONTENTS

UNIT 1

THE SCRIPTS PEOPLE LIVE BY

Have you ever worked with people who:

- are successful in their personal and professional lives and pace themselves for good health?

- frequently perform in failure-oriented ways, often getting criticized, rejected, or injured, pacing themselves for poor health?

- are plodders, working and working but seeming to be stuck in a rut, going around in circles, not curing what could be cured?

If you have, you've probably seen people acting out their psychological scripts — their life plans. These personal scripts can be constructive, destructive, or going nowhere.

SCRIPTS ARE LIFE PLANS

Eric Berne defines a *psychological script* as "an ongoing program, developed in early childhood under parental influence, which directs the individual's behavior in the most important aspects of his life." [1] A psychological script is much like a theatrical script. It provides the life "drama" which a person may be unaware of but still feels compelled to follow. The script is like a blueprint for the shape one's life will take. Even if the plan is not well drawn or the script well written, it dictates what a person feels is "right" to do. It motivates the "show" a person feels compelled to put on. Even if it's a poor show, a person may accept it as the *only* show and feel helpless or unwilling to change it.

There are three basic types of scripts—winning, losing, and going nowhere. Some people have scripts that motivate them to realize their greatest potentials. People with this type of script receive messages, make decisions, and have experiences in early childhood that give them a basic confidence about themselves, strengthening their natural resources. As a consequence, they live according to a constructive, *winning* script. People who treat themselves and others in a humane fashion, who set reasonable goals and achieve them, and who are willing to take responsibility for their own good health demonstrate many winning ways.

Other people may receive messages and make decisions that cause them to live unsatisfying or very unhappy lives. These people drudge along being bored and unhappy and making the same mistakes over and over. They seem stuck, fearful of new things and ideas or fearful that change might make them worse. Stuck in a rut, such people follow *nonwinning* or *going-nowhere* scripts. These people expect others to solve their problems and often do not take personal responsibility for many areas of their lives, including their health.

Still other people receive such negative messages from significant authority figures or have such terrifying childhood experiences that at best they end in failure, at worst in self-destruction. Such people follow *loser* scripts. Some of their "loser" behavior, such as overdosing on drugs or ignoring obvious physical symptoms, may cause them to end up as emergency cases in a doctor's office or hospital. These people often see themselves as victimized, unable to be a positive force in their own lives and may instead undermine or sabotage themselves by doing things that do not support their own good.

SCRIPTS ARE DRAMAS

The reason a psychological script bears such a striking resemblance to a theatrical script is because it has a cast of characters, dialogue, acts, scenes, themes, and plots which move toward a climax and end with a final curtain. The story line may call for excitement and achievement, for boredom and passivity, or for depression and failure. The stage directions are provided by parental messages. These directions may be positive or negative or a combination of both. They may be verbal or nonverbal, consistent or inconsistent. In response to the directions, people choose to comply to the scripting or to rebel against it. [2]

The dramatic themes of personal scripts can be found in children's stories. They often resemble folklore ("Like George Washington, I cannot tell a lie"), mythology ("Atlas isn't the only one who carries the world on his shoulders"), popular TV shows ("Everyone expects me to come to their rescue like Superman"), or a favorite childhood story such as Cinderella ("Some day, someone will rescue me from all this") or Robin Hood ("It's great robbing from the rich and giving to the poor").

A person's story is "rewritten" and rehearsed in a more sophisticated version in adolescence, and the show usually goes on the road when a person enters the early twenties. In fact, any person's script will be related to three basic questions: Who am I? What am I doing here? Who are all those other people? [3]

SCRIPTING STARTS IN CHILDHOOD

Parents and other significant authority figures are the original producers and directors of children's psychological dramas. Important in the formation of a script are the early "messages" and instructions that children receive. Some children are wanted; some are not. At birth they may be accepted or rejected because of social or financial circumstances and such things as sex, appearance, color, or size. Even the circumstances of birth—pain, cost, inconvenience, family relationships, attitudes of relatives (including in-laws)—affect the attitudes and actions parents take toward their children.

Whether born at home or in the hospital, infants, almost as if they had radar, begin to pick up verbal and nonverbal messages about themselves and their worth through their first experiences of being touched or being ignored by others. Infants who are cuddled affectionately, smiled at, and talked to receive messages that are likely to direct them toward constructive life dramas. Touch that implies "You are here, you are important, and we are here to help you" helps to build winning scripts. The recent trend toward natural childbirth, with emotional support and the presence of the family, emphasizes this. [4] Yet some infants are treated as objects rather than as new people. Those who are handled with fright, hostility, or extreme anxiety or who are left alone for extended periods of time are likely to get messages that lead to going-nowhere or destructive life dramas.

These messages contribute to children's self-images and eventually lead to the adoption of dramatic roles. Another way children learn what roles they are expected to play is by the names or nicknames they are given. Someone named "Solomon" may be expected to be wise; "Fatso" may be programmed to always be thinking of food. Role expectations are further strengthened when parents encourage their children to copy a particular person, such as a grandparent, a favorite aunt or uncle, a biblical character, a national hero, a famous movie star, or an infamous news character. For better or worse, the way children respond to parents' expectations molds their future roles and contributes to positive or negative self-images.

Children continue to develop their scripts as they begin to overhear and understand the scripting messages that authority figures put into words, such as,

"That kid is going to be able to do anything she sets her mind to." In response, this child may set high goals that are achievable or high goals that are unrealistic.

Having frequently heard, "You'll never amount to anything," a person may fail in school, be chronically ill, get a poorly paid job, and "never quite make it." Whether their parent figures' instructions are negative or positive, people tend to follow them and to fulfill their expectations.

Important parts of every script are the issues around health and illness. When a little girl frequently hears from a doting parent, "She's always been so frail," that little girl could unnecessarily follow a lifetime of overanxiety and low self-expectation. When a little boy frequently hears, "Big boys don't cry," his script may call for the "being strong" role. To play the role he may suppress his feeling, deny his pain, and resist seeking medical help.

Taking care of one's body, ignoring it, or abusing it becomes part of a life plan. Unfortunately, few people in our culture have scripts that teach them to love and to take care of their bodies. This contempt for the body was true of seven-year-old Tommy, who frequently claimed to hate his skinny arms and short legs. Tommy had regular checkups, yet often went to the school nurse at recess, complaining of "knots" in his stomach and not wanting to go outside to play. In taking a closer look at the situation, the nurse discovered that Tommy's father expected him to be a great ball player and that his older brother was a "star" on the high school football team. Tommy's self-image as a sportsman was so low that he had stomach aches to avoid the stressful situation.

Scripts contain not only compulsions about health, but also directions about vocational choice. Many health care providers choose their professional roles to fit their individual scripts. These scripts call for them to choose their cast of characters and to play their dramatic roles even though they may not be conscious of doing so. [5,6] For example, Ms. Sloan was not aware that she had selected her script at age seven after helping to "nurse" her cancer-ridden mother. Like many children, she felt both sad and mad when her mother died. She also felt a childlike guilt for some of her negative thoughts about her mother and her inability to save her. To protect herself against this negative awareness, she decided to be a nurse so that she could "save" people. Eventually, she chose to work in a hospice for terminally ill patients whom she could not save. With each patient she would start out imagining herself a potential savior. Then each time one died, she felt sad, mad, and guilty once more, thus reinforcing her old role and her old feelings of helplessness. Once again she failed.

EXERCISE 1. YOU AND YOUR SCRIPT

To begin to understand elements of your script, work through the following questions:

What were the implications of your name or other things you were called?

Did you pattern yourself after any particular person?

Say in a sentence what you imagine each of your parent figures thought of you when you were a child.

- What did *you* think of yourself then?

- How does this relate to your self-image now?

- How is your current self-image related to your parents' opinion of you as a child?

- Does your self-appraisal reflect a script of a winner? _____ A Loser? _____ Or someone who is going nowhere? _____

If you continue doing what you're doing now, where and how will you end up?

FAMILIES HAVE SCRIPTS

Individual scripts are usually designed within a family context. Many families have traditional expectations for the life goals, roles, and social status of their members. For example, "My son, the doctor" is a strong expectation in many families. In contrast, "My son, the nurse" is a rare expectation.

Families script children toward health care vocations when their expectations show in comments such as:

"We've had a surgeon in our family for five generations."

"Our lot in life is to clean up other people's dirty messes."

"What a nurse you'd be! Just like Aunt Suzy and Aunt Ruth."

"You should be a dentist like your father and grandfather."

"Members of our family have always been leaders in medical research."

"Sacrificing for others is the most noble occupation a person can have."

When these scripting messages are said with affection and caring, children may comply. When they are overstated, children may rebel. As Sam reported, "I probably would have gone to med school if my parents hadn't nagged me day after day after day on the same subject." Nagging or criticism often elicits procrastination or rebellion. Thus well-intentioned parents may interfere with their children's need to choose for themselves.

Not all parents are that well intentioned. Some frequently use an epithet like "You no-good kid." A rebellious offspring may finish med school with honors just to prove parents wrong. The script theme becomes "I'll show you."

In addition to vocational scripting, families often have traditional expectations about specific diseases or injuries. This was true of the Peters family. Suzy, age eight, had had a broken ankle. Les, age twelve, broke his leg skiing. Mom and Dad had had multiple fractures when their motorcycle hit a pole. Grandma had fallen off a ladder twice, breaking her thumb and her collarbone. They all frequently laughed about being "accident-prone."

Families also have expectations about *how to act* when ill or in pain. For example, some are taught to always seek help, whereas others don't dare to admit that they need it. Sally Anderson's family forbade illness. She was severely reprimanded for any physical complaint. "We Andersons are a hardy lot and certainly don't waste our money on doctors." When Sally developed severe intestinal pain, she waited two days before seeking help. In fact, a good friend had to insist that she go to a hospital. Later she told her friend that a part of her intestine had "died" and that she had just made it to the hospital in time. Many people like Sally have difficulty recognizing and admitting to life-threatening situations.

EXERCISE 2. PARENTAL SCRIPT MESSAGES

This exercise is not intended for an in-depth personal survey, but rather as a general discussion to help you begin to discover how scripts are formed and how they later impact a person's life. Discuss what messages parents might send about the following issues and then how a person might learn to think, feel, and behave as a result. Also consider whether the messages typically would be the same for both boys and girls.

working hard   staying clean

getting educated   being masculine

being religious   being feminine

achieving success	cleaning one's plate
having brains	developing talents
being attractive or ugly	enjoying one's body
being healthy	being an achiever or a nonachiever
helping others	being sick

You may now want to explore what messages *you* received from each of your parent figures about each of the issues above.

EXERCISE 3. FAMILY SCRIPTS FOR LIFE WORK

Is your choice of occupation in any way tied to a family expectation or tradition?

- If so, what are the pluses for you?

- The minuses?

- If not, were there other significant people in your life who encouraged you?

- What are the pluses for you?

• The minuses?

ORGANIZATIONS HAVE SCRIPTS

Like people and families, organizations too follow scripts. [7] Organizational scripts are the patterns that give an organization its identity and that often determine its destiny. They include the ongoing program for the success, failure, or "treading water" story line of the organization's progress. Just like people, some organizations seem destined for success; some seem destined to fail; and some seem to go nowhere.

The essence of every organizational script is its theme. A few common themes some hospitals or clinics emulate are: being the biggest, being the poorest, being the best, being ahead of the times, having the highest quality, being the most exclusive, going downhill.

Organizational scripts and their themes include the institutionalized injunctions and permissions regarding expectations from all levels of employment, the built-in rewards for approval and status along with the built-in punishments, and the formalized lines of communication—which are, all too often, only downward. In addition, the script usually contains expectations about such things as sex roles, grooming and dress, personal conduct, and working hours.

The personal scripts of an organization's founder (or founders) have a profound effect on the organizational script. In the beginning, patterns are established verbally and nonverbally in written policies and unwritten expectations. Some founders, even years after their demise, sit like ghosts at today's conference table or on the board, wielding an eerie influence over present decisions. Others set up their organization to self-destruct when they die. They delegate no authority, share few responsibilities, covet the records, and literally leave things so that no one can take over effectively. Others, by contrast, create a situation that can be modified and built on. It is often this capacity to change that determines the survival possibilities of an organization.

In one mental health organization the organizational script reflected many aspects of the personal script of its founder. Following his sudden death, his portrait was prominently displayed over the speaker's podium at the semiannual conferences. This practice continued for ten years.

Many executives and managers, both junior and senior, often remain committed to the original organizational scripts and may be advanced on the basis of how well they "fit the mold" and meet the founder's expectations. They do not evaluate patterns that may have brought success or failure in the past with the realities of change in today's world. Such a situation usually creates tension.

In one instance the nursing service in a small hospital had been given the script injunction from its founder to take care of the patients' families as well as the patients. When the hospital moved and increased from 100 beds to 487 beds,

new departments were established with larger scope and responsibility. New personnel were hired. This caused great difficulty for those on the nursing staff, who now saw other helpers, such as social workers, as threats to their jobs and authority. Though dependent on these new departments, they resented and were suspicious of them.

In another small hospital, founded by a religious group, the script theme was clearly "Save others before taking care of yourself." As a consequence, employees were expected to be available at any hour of any day. They were to put their professional lives above everything else. When workers began dropping their "Good Samaritan" stance and demanding union standards, the hospital administration was baffled. To keep things as they were, the administration even attempted to arouse guilt with such comments as, "No one seems to care around here any more!"

Inflexibility in organizations, as in people, stops the flow of the natural course of growth and development. It blocks the awareness of current trends and demands. For example, some health care settings may find it difficult to adapt to the current trend among many people to seek alternatives to traditional treatment or to take more care of and to make more choices for themselves.

Just as organizations have scripts, so too do groups or subcultures within them. As a result, a particular unit within an organization can have a subcultural script. It can have its own goals, rituals, topics of conversation, and even its own language. A common problem between units is poor lateral communication. For example, housekeeping may have poor communication with dietetics. Making changes often means opening up lateral communication lines with a common, nontechnical language that doesn't define some people as "in" and OK and some as "out" and not-OK.

EXERCISE 4. RECOGNIZING AN ORGANIZATIONAL SCRIPT

When your organization was established, what were the goals, expectations, and policies around:

- patient care

- administration policies

- staffing procedures

- the physical plant

Are these same expectations present today?

If so, are they healthy and appropriate?

If not, have the changes been productive?

How do you see the people who founded your organization still affecting it?

How is your group like a subculture? If so, how does it help or hinder good communication?

Does the subculture show because of the language used, schedules utilized, clothes worn, or what?

EXERCISE 5. THE SCRIPT IN ACTION

The direction in which a script is going can often be recognized by repetitive, non-changing patterns of the people involved. Consider your organization:

- What keeps happening over and over again?

- Is what happens productive?

- Is what happens destructive?

- Is what happens going nowhere?

- How would you summarize the organizational script where you work as it is currently being acted out?

- If your organization keeps going as it is now, how will it end up?

EXERCISE 6: DIAGNOSING THE HEALTH OF AN ORGANIZATION

Like people, organizations may be healthy or unhealthy. In this exercise have a little fun in the way you see your organization by imagining it as a person being diagnosed. What are signs of its health?

If your organization had a physical disorder, what would it be— e.g., high blood pressure, anemia, epilepsy, ulcers, constipation, or what?

Disease   *Symptoms*   *Prognosis*

What would help to bring about some possible "cures"?

Now ask these same questions about your immediate work environment.

Do you see any connections?

CULTURAL SCRIPTS AFFECT HEALTH CARE

In addition to individuals' and organizations' having scripts, even larger groups have dramatic expectations. For instance, the accepted and expected dramatic patterns that occur within a whole society are called cultural scripts. They are determined by the spoken and unspoken assumptions believed by the majority of people within that group about expected roles, stage directions, costumes, settings, and final curtains. Cultural scripts reflect what is thought of as the "national character," and some groups repeat the same drama generation after generation.

Cultural scripts usually dictate specific roles. For example, most cultures differentiate—rationally or irrationally—between the roles men are to play and the roles expected of women. [8,9] In the United States, for example, doctors traditionally have been male and nurses female. Doctors have had the knowledge and power to make the diagnoses and to prescribe treatments. Nurses have carried out orders, administered medication, cared for patients, and overseen details. But today many of these scripts are being changed. Both physicians and nurses may be either male or female. [10] Services formerly performed only by physicians are now being performed by nurse practitioners, paramedics, and technicians of both sexes. In addition, many nurses today are assigned to planning and administrative work instead of direct patient care. Some nurses like the challenge; others complain of being overwhelmed by paperwork and having little time for peer and patient contact. When traditional scripts are challenged, some confusion and frustration are bound to result.

Even the food people eat or refuse to eat is culturally scripted. One woman from Mexico, recovering from an accident in the United States, complained that the hospital food was worse than the broken bones. "There's no seasoning, no onions. It all tastes the same. Like mush. I've got to get out of here just to get something decent to eat." (Of course, many other people have agreed with this last complaint!)

Public health nurses and other health care professionals who go to people's homes to offer care often need to be aware of the cultural traditions of their clients. For example, elderly Mr. Sanchez, recovering from a stroke, felt humiliated when unable to pull up a chair for the visiting nurse. And Ms. Lee, on a welfare budget and convalescing from a serious accident, was very apologetic for not being able to offer tea and sesame cookies, "the way we *always* did it back home."

Most cultures have favorite expected foods, common postures and gestures, rituals, sexual behaviors, and manners which individuals in the group tend to comply with or rebel against. Even basic philosophical beliefs about illness and wellness can have a cultural flavor. For example, one traditional approach to Western medicine has been that disease is alleviated by the technology of a "cure"—perhaps surgery, radiation, or a drug. One traditional Eastern approach to health is that disease represents an energy imbalance and that before a cure can be effected, a realignment of that energy balance must take place. Wellness clinics and holistic-medicine approaches often integrate the Eastern philosophy along with Western tradition.

EXERCISE 7. CULTURAL SCRIPTS

Think about your personal cultural scripting.

- Does your cultural heritage affect your attitudes about sickness and wellness in any way today? For example, who deserves treatment or who doesn't? What should be done when someone is ill? Which kinds of illnesses are OK to talk about and which are not? Who has the power to give treatment and how?

- Think of at least one thing you do now related to health care or illness that is culturally determined. For example, what are the rituals of the members of your culture around childbirth?   How do they take care of themselves? How do they attend the sick?

- Think of the drama patterns about nutrition, exercise, getting colds, having fevers, managing stress, etc., that were in the culture you grew up in. For example, did you come from a long line of people who ate quantities of pasta, pastries, meats, rice, soybeans, vegetables, fruits,—what? Did your traditions call for a day of rest? Were your people expected to clean their plates to save the starving children elsewhere?

- Does your cultural scripting around health seem to be constructive, destructive, or going nowhere, or a mixture?

- Now discuss how cultural scripts affect the attitudes of health care recipients.

LIFE POSITIONS AFFECT SCRIPTS

People's gut-level sense of OKness or not-OKness profoundly affects how they work together and how they take care of themselves and others. Their deep feelings about their own worth develop very early in life. People also formulate ideas about the worth of others. They do this by crystallizing their experiences and making decisions about what life means, what parts they are going to play, and how they are going to act out the parts in their life dramas. These are days of decision [11] —the time when they commit themselves, *without awareness,* to acting in certain ways that become part of their characters. Decisions made early in life about oneself and others may be quite unrealistic, although they seem logical and make sense at the time.

For example, people who are ridiculed and frequently called stupid may agree, yet at the same time conclude that other people are smart and know everything. They base their scripts on the position "I'm not-OK, but other people are OK." They may fail, feeling that they have no brains and can't do anything right.

Such early decisions are the basis for life positions. These positions, even if negative, are crystallized, often subconsciously, into script roles. For example, a person who has a deep feeling of I'm not-OK and You're OK may say to a co-worker, "Gee, you seem to be able to do everything right the first time. Look at me. I still can't do it well" or (whining), "Why do things like this always happen to me? You never seem to have this kind of trouble" or, "I'm stupid! How can you stand putting up with me?"

When taking positions about themselves, people may conclude:

I can't think for myself.	I'm as good as anybody else.
I do everything wrong.	I do many things right.
I don't deserve to live.	I have a good head on my shoulders.

When taking positions about others, a person may conclude:

People are wonderful.	People are out to get me.
People are basically honest.	People are no darn good.
People will help me.	People can't be trusted.

The positions above can be generalized: "I'm OK" or "I'm not-OK" and "You're OK" or "You're not-OK." They fit together to form the four basic life positions. [12]

The first position, "I'm OK, You're OK," is the *confident position.* It is held by people who are mentally healthy. If realistic, people with this position can solve their problems constructively. Their expectations are likely to be valid. They accept the significance of people. They assume responsibility for their own health whenever possible. For example, they might ask, "What preventive measures do you recommend for me?" They also help others to do the same: "This diet and exercise program should increase your energy."

The second position, "I'm OK, You're not-OK," is the *superiority position.* This is the position of bossy persons who criticize and blame others for mistakes. They may be overauthoritarian, conveying attitudes such as: "I'm the doctor; I know best." "I'm the nurse; don't ask questions." "I'm the technician; do as I say." "I'm the housekeeper; I know the solution." "I'm the dietician; eat what I say." "I'm the patient. I'm paying the bills, so come when I call."

The third position, "I'm not-OK, You're OK," is the *anxious position.* This is common with persons who feel inadequate when they compare themselves with others. It leads them to withdraw, to experience depression, and in severe cases to become self-destructive. If patients perceive health care providers from an anxious position, they often have "superperson" expectations of them while feeling inadequate themselves. They may unthinkingly yield their personal responsibility to others: "You know I can't think straight, so just do what you think I need."

The fourth position, "I'm not-OK, You're not-OK," is the *hopeless position.* This is the position of people who lose interest in living. They give up on themselves and others and may require extensive psychological care. In extreme cases, they may resort to suicide and/or homicide. [13,14] The attitude is: "No matter what either of us does, it's not going to make any difference."

EXERCISE 8. LIFE POSITIONS AND ATTITUDES

Discuss in small groups how people might in childhood take life positions that would later affect their attitudes toward health care providers.

- I'm OK and You're OK

- I'm OK and You're not-OK

- I'm not-OK and You're OK

- I'm not-OK and You're not-OK

EXERCISE 9. LIFE POSITIONS IN HEALTH CARE

Discuss in small groups how health care providers might act out the following life positions toward a client who has come for services. Select a specific person, e.g., clerk, M.D., R.N., L.V.N., technician, P.H.M., H.S.A., etc., who is represented in your work group. Also select a setting, e.g., office, clinic, hospital, convalescent home, etc.

How might a health care provider act when feeling:

* *Anxious*: I'm not-OK and You're OK

* *Superior:* I'm OK and You're not-OK

* *Hopeless*: I'm not-OK and You're not-OK

* *Confident:* I'm OK and You're OK

SUMMARY

Individual, family, cultural, and organizational scripts intertwine to form intricate dramas affecting the lives and health of many people. The acts people learn to put on and to participate in form parts of these dramas.

People in health care who have an awareness of scripts have the advantage of being able to identify constructive, destructive, or going-nowhere patterns both in individuals and in groups. They can recognize that these patterns are by choice and that therefore they can be scrutinized and corrected or reversed to serve people more productively.

Since scripts tend to feel "right," they are difficult to change until people know that they have them. Awareness through a transactional analysis (TA) approach helps people see more clearly what is going on. Heightened awareness offers the option of more autonomy. People don't have to be stuck in a system that isn't working for them. They can choose to change many negative aspects of the variety of life dramas they're caught up in. As health care professionals, they can broaden their perspective as well as enhance their winning ways.

UNIT 2
PERSONALITIES PEOPLE DEVELOP

Have you worked with someone who:

- points an accusing finger at others as parents often do?

- continually takes care of others in a parental way?

- acts reasonable and collects facts before making decisions?

- throws temper tantrums like a little child?

- never interrupts, having been trained as a child to "be seen but not heard"?

If so, you have seen the three ego states in action. These ego states—the Parent ego state, the Adult ego state, and the Child ego state—form the structure of personality.

EVERYONE HAS THREE EGO STATES

Eric Berne defines an ego state as "a consistent pattern of feeling and experience directly related to a corresponding consistent pattern of behavior." [1] The implications are that what happens to people is recorded in their brains and nervous tissue. These recordings include everything that people experience in childhood, all that they incorporate from their parent figures, their perceptions of events, their feelings associated with these events, and the distortions they bring to their memories. As though stored on video tape, these recordings can be replayed and the event recalled and even reexperienced.

Each person has three ego states, which can be separate and distinct sources of behavior: the Parent ego state, the Adult ego state, and the Child ego state. These are not abstract concepts, but realities. "Parent, Adult, and Child represent real people who now exist or who once existed, who have legal names and civic identities." [2]

The structure of personality is diagrammed as follows:

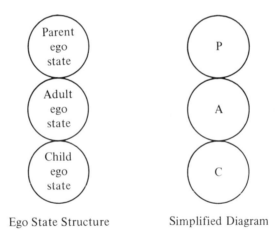

Ego State Structure   Simplified Diagram

Ego states are colloquially termed Parent, Adult, and Child. When capitalized in this workbook, they will refer to ego states, not to actual parents, adults, or children.

The *Parent ego state* contains the attitudes and behavior incorporated from external sources, primarily parents. Messages from institutions, churches, schools, and society also impact it. Outwardly, the Parent ego state is often expressed toward others in prejudicial, critical, and nurturing behavior. Inwardly, it is experienced as old Parent messages which continue to be "heard" in our heads and to influence the inner Child.

The *Adult ego state* is not related to a person's age. Rather, it is oriented to current reality and to the objective gathering of information. With the Adult, a person organizes, is adaptable and intelligent, and functions by testing reality, estimating probabilities, and computing dispassionately.

The *Child ego state* contains all of the impulses that come naturally to infants. It also contains the recordings of their early experiences, how they responded to them, and the "positions" they took about themselves and others. It is expressed as "old" or archaic behavior from childhood.

When you are acting, thinking, and feeling as you observed your parents to be doing, your psychic energy is in your Parent ego state.

When you are dealing with current reality, gathering facts, and computing objectively, your psychic energy is in your Adult ego state.

When you are feeling and acting as you did when you were a child, your psychic energy is in your Child ego state.

Psychic energy flows from one ego state to another. And at any given time one ego state may be more "charged" than the other two. For example, when people come for treatment, they are often feeling fearful and in the Child ego state. When they write a check in payment, they may compute their bank balance with the rational Adult ego state. When they show sympathy or disapproval, they are often acting from the nurturing or judgmental aspects of their Parent ego state.

People's bodies, emotions, and intellectual skills move at different speeds. Adjusting this speed to a situation is often difficult. Some people find it hard to "slow down." Others have difficulty when they try to "hurry up."

In some highly effective people, the flow of energy may be quite rapid. People whose free energy moves rapidly may be exciting and stimulating, yet others may have difficulty keeping up with the fast-moving pace. In others it may be slow, yet they will also be effective. People whose energy moves more slowly are those who are slow to start and slow to stop how they act, how they feel, and how they think. Their responses may be of high quality, although other people may become impatient with such slowness.

This happened to Lee, for many years a nurse in geriatrics. Lee had unknowingly slowed down to be more effective with older patients. When suddenly transferred to the ward for adolescents, Lee felt very uncomfortable at the "fast pace" that was expected and the criticism received for being "slower than molasses." Brocard, whom Lee replaced, had the opposite experience. Brocard had been accustomed to responding quickly with a ready wit to some rather volatile adolescents who enjoyed it. When transferred to the pulmonary unit, Brocard's fast-thinking Child ego state was not appreciated. Witty remarks often led patients to laugh and then to cough painfully. If these two nurses had known about the dynamics of energy flow in ego states, they might have adjusted to their new positions with more understanding and less frustration and confusion.

EXERCISE 1. EGO STATE REACTION QUIZ

Identify each reaction to the situation as Parent, Adult, or Child (P, A, or C). There will be one of each in each situation. Naturally these will be educated guesses, since you can't hear the tone of voice or see the gestures.

1. A clerk loses an important medical record.

   a) "Why can't you keep track of anything you're responsible for?" ____

   b) "Check each person who may have used it in the last two days and try to trace it. Perhaps Mrs. Smith can help you." ____

   c) "I can't solve your problems. I didn't take your old record." ____

2. An X-ray machine breaks down.

   a) "See if a repairman can come this morning." ____

   b) "Wow! This machine is always breaking down. I'd like to throw it on the floor and jump on it." ____

   c) "Those operators are so careless. They should know better." ____

3. A secretary defends a letter written in response to a confusing memo.

   a) "Golly, Dr. Smith, I read that memo three times, and it's so bad I just can't figure it out. He must be a jerk." ____

    b) "I found the memo contradictory, Dr. Smith. I'd appreciate your telling me what you see as his main question." ____

    c) "We shouldn't have to answer this memo at all. That man clearly doesn't know what he's talking about." ____

4. Coffee-break rumors report that a nurse is about to be transferred.

    a) "Boy, tell me more. I'd like to get something on old Pratchet. What a pain in the neck!" ____

    b) "Let's not spread a story that may not be true. If we have a question, let's ask the boss." ____

    c) "We really shouldn't talk about someone who has so many troubles—financial, marital, you name it." ____

5. An administrator has had an important proposal rejected.

    a) "Poor Mr. Fuji, you must feel terrible. I'll fix you a cup of tea to cheer you up." ____

    b) "You think you feel bad! Just listen to what happened to me!" ____

    c) "I'm sorry about the reversal, Mr. Fuji. Let me know if there is anything you want me to do." ____

6. An entry-level employee appears on the job in hiking shorts.

    a) "Wow, look at that!" ____

    b) "Shorts should not be allowed in the office." ____

    c) "I wonder why those were chosen to wear to work." ____

7. A staff nurse is appointed supervisor.

    a) "Well, Mrs. Murphy deserved it. After all, with all those children to feed, she needs that extra money. Poor thing." ____

    b) "Oh, brother! She got that for buttering up the higher-ups." ____

    c) "I thought I was more qualified for the promotion than Mrs. Murphy. But maybe I haven't given her enough credit." ____

8. An additional lab technician position is denied by budget restraints.

    a) "How will we manage the work load?" ____

    b) "This stinking clinic isn't worth working for anyway." ____

    c) "I believe that they should cut out one of those assistant supervisors. It's just one more person not carrying a full share of the work load." ____

EXERCISE 2. ANALYZING EGO STATE VOCABULARY AND BODY LANGUAGE

People use words, postures, and so forth that can be observed as coming from different ego states. This exercise will heighten your awareness of these differences.

Parent Ego State

List words or phrases —for example, "should," "they must," "don't worry"— that seem to come from the Parent ego states of the people you work with.

List gestures, postures, tones of voice, facial expressions, etc., that reflect the Parent ego state.

Adult Ego State

List words or phrases—for example, "probably," "estimate," "how much?"— that reflect the Adult ego state.

List gestures, postures, tones of voice, facial expressions, etc., that appear to be from the adult ego state.

Child Ego State

List words or phrases—for example, "wow," "ouch!" "nuts to you"—that demonstrate the Child ego state.

List gestures, postures, tones of voice, facial expressions, etc., that show the Child ego state.

Note: A few suggested responses are noted in Appendix B.

EVERYONE HAS A PARENT EGO STATE

The Parent ego state is the incorporation of the attitudes and behavior of all emotionally significant people who serve as parent figures to the child. It does not necessarily function in ways culturally defined as "motherly" or "fatherly."

For better or for worse, it is not uncommon for health care personnel to be expected to serve as substitute parents. They may meet the expectation and act that way: nurturing, critical, controlling, indifferent, inconsistent, supportive, punitive, and so forth. Some patients reinforce this. Just the thought of seeing a doctor or nurse moves their energy into the Child ego state, and they then project onto others their childhood experiences with authority figures.

Some health care persons prefer to communicate in parental ways; others resent being seen as all-responsible authority figures. It becomes apparent that the interplay of people's ego states strongly influences the quality and direction of their transactions.

The Parent Ego State Is Expressed Outwardly

When a Parent ego state is expressed outwardly, people transact with the ego states of others as they observed their own parents doing.

Outward Expression of
the Parent Ego State

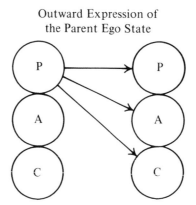

For example, when Mr. Wylie chaired the meeting, he tapped his pencil on the table to make his point, just as he'd seen his father do; later he patted someone on the back in congratulations, again copying his father. At the same meeting a competent woman who wanted to speak up sat silently, just as she had seen her mother do in groups of people. Knowledge of habitual behavior helps people decide when such behavior is appropriate and when new responses are called for.

The Parent Ego State Is Expressed Inwardly

People not only act toward others as their parents did, but also hear parental messages in their heads. These messages are similar to video tape recordings. They are experienced as an inner dialogue and are usually heard by the Child. It is important to personal effectiveness that the Adult become aware of this dialogue and its consequences.

Inward Influence of the
Parent Ego State

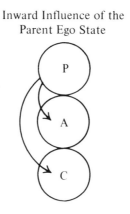

Some Parent-type messages are encouraging. Some are not. The inner message may be permissive, confusing, supportive, condemning, or rigidly moralistic. For example, one man asked to present a point of view at a meeting heard an old Parent tape: "Don't make a fool of yourself in front of other people." In contrast, a woman at the same meeting, when asked to make a presentation, heard her father's words of encouragement: "Don't be afraid to give it a try." These messages had very different consequences.

Parents Exhibit Nurturing and Critical Behavior

Parents may be sympathetic, protective, and nurturing on some occasions and critical, prejudicial, moralizing, or disciplining on others. Some parents tend to be more nurturing than judgmental, whereas others are more judgmental than nurturing. When children have nurturing parents, they develop a Parent ego state of their own that contains nurturing behavior. If they have critical parents, they are likely to be critical at times.

The Parent ego state is filled with opinions and prejudices about such things as religion, politics, traditions, sexual roles, life styles, child rearing, proper dress, ways of speech, cold remedies, proper nutrition, etc. A person acting from the critical side of the Parent may come on as a bossy know-it-all whose behavior intimidates the Child in other people. A boss, peer, patient, professional, or friend who uses the critical Parent too frequently usually irritates other people and can even alienate them.

Whereas some patients who do not feel physically or emotionally well want to be parented, others prefer a more informational, adult approach. For example, one patient about to have office surgery may prefer hearing a parental "Now just relax, we're going to take good care of you," whereas another may prefer a factual "You have a fifty-fifty chance of this problem's being corrected."

Ego States Within the Parent

Each parent figure has three unique ego states. Consequently, a person's own Parent ego state is likely to incorporate his or her parents' Parent, Adult, and Child, the babysitter's Parent, Adult, and Child, and so forth. At times parents behave toward their children as their parents behaved toward them—moralizing, punishing, nurturing, ignoring. At other times parents reason on the basis of current, objective data—explaining why, demonstrating how, searching for facts, and solving problems. Other times they use behavior from their own childhood—whining, withdrawing, frolicking, giggling, manipulating, and playing. Therefore, the behavior of a person responding from the Parent ego state may stem from any ego state incorporated from one or more parent figures. The Parent in a person's Parent ego state is most often the grandparents.

Analyzing the ego states within an ego state is called *second-order structural analysis.* [3] Applied to the Parent, this means sorting out the Parent, Adult, and Child ego states within the person's Parent ego state. For example, the following story illustrates how certain traditions in a family script may be transmitted, although the reasons behind them are long forgotten.

A bride served baked ham, and her husband asked why she had cut the ends off. "Well, that's the way mother always did it," she replied. The next time his mother-in-law stopped by, he asked her why she cut the ends off the hams. "That's the way my mother did it," she replied. And when grandma visited, she too was asked why she sliced the ends off. She said, "That's the only way I could get it into the pan."

In the same way, many health care beliefs and practices—some useful, some out of date—are generations old, passed on from Parent to Parent. "Old wives' tales" may not coincide with standard medical practice of today, but may still have a grain of truth which represents the wisdom of the ages. Chicken soup, often joked about, actually helps some people get well. It helps break up phlegm and soothes raw mucus membranes. Scientists at New York's Mt. Sinai Hospital label it "efficacious upper respiratory tract infection therapy." [4]

EXERCISE 3. RECOGNIZING PARENTAL BEHAVIOR

The Parent ego state often employs critical messages, such as, "You always mess up on following instructions." What are three typical *critical* Parental messages that health care providers commonly use?

How effective are these messages to good communication?

The Parent ego state often employs nurturing messages—protective, sympathetic, "taking care of" messages, such as, "Take a little nap and you'll feel better." What are three typical *nurturing* Parental statements that health care providers commonly use?

How effective are these to good communication?

The Parent ego state often employs controlling messages, sometimes disguised as nurturing, such as, "We know what's best for us, don't we?" (Then the person proceeds to take total charge.) What are three typical *controlling* Parental statements that health care providers commonly use?

How effective are these to good communication?

EXERCISE 4. YOUR PARENT EGO STATE AT WORK

For each of your parent figures, list three important Parent messages you still hear in your head:

Figure out from which ego state in your Parent the messages came from.

- Are they family traditions that came from your parents' Parent?

- Are they statements of probability that came from your parents' Adult?

- Are they emotional responses that came from your parents' Child?

List three Parent traditions or opinions about illness or treatment that you learned from your parents and still use:

List how your Parent ego state shows at work:

Now study the lists above and ask yourself: "In what way is my Parent ego state an asset to me on the job? In what ways does it interfere?"

EVERYONE HAS A CHILD EGO STATE

The child he or she was still lingers in every person. Within all people are the permanent recordings of early life. These recordings include the ways they *experienced* the world, the ways they *felt* about the world they experienced, and the ways they *adapted* to it. When people respond as they did when they were little—inquisitive, affectionate, selfish, mean, playful, whining, manipulative—they are responding from the Child ego state.

The Child ego state has three discernable parts—the Natural Child, the Little Professor, and the Adapted Child.

The Natural Child Is Uncensored

The Natural Child is the very young, impulsive, untrained, expressive infant still inside each person. It is often like a self-centered, pleasure-loving baby responding with cozy affection when needs are met or with angry rebellion when needs are not met. The Natural Child within each person's Child ego state is what a baby would be "naturally" without other influences—affectionate, impulsive, sensuous, uncensored, and curious. The Natural Child is also fearful, self-indulgent, self-centered, rebellious, and aggressive.

Strong basic drives, related to physical survival, are centered in the Natural Child. Probably the strongest basic drive in most people is the urge to live. [5] When treating patients, health care persons count on this urge and, when appropriate, reinforce it with words of hope, aware that the person without hope has given up and is less likely to get well. Yet in some people the Natural Child is so repressed that it is almost blocked off, releasing little energy for the healing process.

Either of these extremes can create problems. Some health care providers are so out of touch with their own Natural Child's needs that they avoid taking care of themselves until they become seriously ill and are forced to recognize the importance of self-care. In others, the Natural Child may rule their lives to the point of narcissistic overindulgence, reflecting an infant's perception of being the center of the universe. Neither of these kinds of people serves as adequate models of responsible self-care to their clients.

EXERCISE 5. RECOGNIZING THE NATURAL CHILD

Describe the ways in which the Natural Child might be expressed in the course of a work day. (If you don't work a day shift, change the times to fit your schedule.)

- Awakening/Prework hours

- On arriving at work

- Morning break

- Late-morning work

- Lunch

- Early afternoon

- Break (or transition period)

- End of work day

- After work

- Dinner

- Evening

- Getting ready for bed

The Little Professor Is Intuitive

The Little Professor is the unschooled wisdom of a child. It is that part of the Child ego state that is intuitive, manipulative, and creative. When intuiting, the Little Professor responds to nonverbal messages and plays hunches. With it a child also figures things out, such as when to cry, when to be quiet, and how to manipulate a parent into smiling.

In later life people might use their Little Professor to manipulate others—to get what they want by acting sad, depressed, hostile, or coy. A supervisor might get sympathy by sighing, "Nobody understands me." A doctor might tell a child, "This shot might hurt, but afterwards you can have a prize from the treasure chest." It's much like "A spoon full of sugar helps the medicine go down."

When people use the Little Professor intuitively and creatively, they may experience moments of insight, for example, when diagnosing a disease that is difficult to recognize. However, a person's Little Professor is not necessarily well informed and often needs the aid of the Adult.

In fact, when the Adult and Little Professor function together, they make a good team. Together they can do such things as design a new pediatric unit, improve human relationships, create a new treatment, or develop new surgical procedures. People seem to "know" much more than they have learned academically. A person may show this inner team work (right brain/left brain integration) with remarks such as:

- "I sense that this is not what's really bothering you."

- "You know, I have a hunch. Let's do some tests."

- "You seem to need the sunshine today. Would you like the shade open?"

The Little Professor also helps to solve problems creatively. When the staff feels frustrated attempting to get things done through "channels," the Little Professor might figure out an alternative route. As one nurse explained, "When a floor is very busy, calling Registration to delay routine admissions is impossible. They won't do it, and odds are that they will call the Nursing Office and complain, thus adding to the busyness if the Nursing Office calls and demands an explanation. A way to get around this is to ask the housekeepers (one definitely has to make friends with the housekeepers, since they are the key in a hospital) to slow down reporting that a room is ready. A little devious maybe, but functional and no one suffers."

EXERCISE 6. RECOGNIZING THE LITTLE PROFESSOR

Describe the ways in which the intuitive, creative, and manipulative Little Professor might be expressed on different jobs by the following:

- Health care attendants or aides

- Nursing staff

- Supervisors

- Administration

- Laboratory staff

- Medical students and technical staff

- Patients

What Little Professor capacities help get the job done?

List Little Professor capacities that help support other staff and patient care

List some that might interfere.

The Adapted Child Is the Trained Child

The Adapted Child is that part of the Child ego state that contains a modification of the Natural Child's inclinations. Adaptations of natural impulses occur in response to traumas, experiences, and training. They also occur because of the expectations of significant authority figures.

One of the earliest adaptations concerns eating. Any child *naturally* wants to eat when hungry. Shortly after birth, however, this natural urge may be modified by a schedule determined by parents or other caretakers. Sometimes this schedule is excessively rigid. For example, in the past some people believed that infants "should be" fed and handled on a four-hour schedule so they "won't get spoiled." When these babies grew into adults, many were not assertive about their needs, believing that needs can be met only on a rigid schedule. Also, some people learn early to adapt to *most* of their needs by eating. Some eventually even learn to believe that their own excessive eating may help less fortunate people elsewhere.

Eric Berne says that the Adapted Child is sometimes like a ventriloquist's dummy because it is likely to do what parents want done whether it is rational or irrational. Whereas some adaptation of natural impulses is essential to function socially, many children experience training that is unnecessarily repressive. As a result, their natural expressiveness becomes overly inhibited. Common adaptations to parental demands are: complying, procrastinating, and rebelling.

People who are overly adapted to comply may shun responsibility by seeking life careers that are routine or in which someone else calls the shots. Overtly these people don't cause dissension.

People who learn to withdraw as an adaptation may seek life careers in which they are isolated from others or rarely speak to others. They don't get involved.

People who adapt by procrastinating find it difficult to meet deadlines. They may not get work done on time and often delay starting a project. They spin their wheels and have a difficult time achieving.

People who adapt by rebelling often have difficulty dealing with legitimate authority in later life. They may refuse to follow orders on the job or may smolder or sulk in response to a request. Some act out by indiscriminately joining movements against the "establishment," and their rebellious acts overshadow their causes.

EXERCISE 7. RECOGNIZING THE ADAPTED CHILD

Describe how the Adapted Child in a patient might be expressed:

	Negatively	*Positively*
• In the emergency room		
• During a physical exam		
• When hearing news of necessary surgery		
• When asked to give up some form of addiction		

EXERCISE 8. YOUR CHILD EGO STATE AT WORK

Think of three situations in which you used Child words or behavior.

Identify which were:

- Adapted Child

- Natural Child

- Little Professor

Were these behaviors appropriate means of communication in that setting? If so, describe how. If not, describe how.

Write three things you do now or would like to do to express your Natural Child at work:

Write three things you do or would like to do to express your Little Professor at work:

Write three things that you do or would like to do to express your Adapted Child at work:

EVERYONE HAS AN ADULT EGO STATE

The Adult ego state can be used to reason dispassionately, to evaluate stimuli, to gather and sort out information, and to store it for future reference. Furthermore, it enables a person to use this information to make choices and to take action. It enables a person to become more independent of past experiences, to be more selective with responses, and to improve ineffective communication patterns. Persons in the Parent also reason, yet often on the basis of tradition. In the Child ego state they are more likely to reason on the basis of feelings.

The Adult can function as a "change agent." It gives people a measure of objectivity so that they can examine themselves more realistically. As a result, they can evaluate Parent and Child programming and decide what is all right for today and what needs to be changed.

By using the Adult, a person can reality-test and estimate probabilities. Reality-testing is the process of checking out what is real. It involves separating fact from fantasy, traditions, opinions, and archaic feelings. It includes perceiving and evaluating current situations and relating the data to past knowledge and experience. Reality-testing allows people to figure out alternative solutions.

When people have alternative solutions, they can then estimate the probable consequences of the various courses of action, thus minimizing the possibility of failure and regret and increasing the possibility of creative success. For example, a professional programmed with "If you want something done right, you better do it yourself" can reality-test this value and decide whether or not it is appropriate. If not, the person can search out new options for such things as delegating staff responsibilities and organizing patients' self-management.

The Adult Can Be the Manager of the Personality

The Adult ego state, as the manager of the personality, takes charge. When this happens, the person no longer assumes the stance of a victim, but instead takes full responsibility for creating her or his own life. When people take charge of their own lives, the Adult becomes a strong ally. If it is flexible and updated with current information, it is like a wise and strong referee in a boxing match. It arbitrates the differences between the Parent and Child ego states, especially if the inner dialogue between the two is hurtful, confusing, or destructive. With positive assertion, it will separate the negative aspects of the Parent and Child and insist on fair play. It looks for the facts, updates information, and becomes a more "fair" Parent to the Child than perhaps the actual parents were able to be—setting rational limits, giving intelligent permissions, and seeking responsible gratifications for the Child.

As the manager of the personality, the Adult examines past traditions and evaluates their current meaning. It also listens to the needs, intuition, and wisdom of the inner Child and responds as a responsible manager would. Just as a good manager looks for the potential and possibilities in people and develops them, the Adult looks for the positive aspects of the Parent and Child to enhance a person's life and also the lives of others. The Adult as manager knows where the buck stops and invests more time in solving problems than in placing blame and making up excuses.

Good managers make their decisions on the best possible information available. Since the Adult ego state is somewhat like a computer, it can be fed misinformation and thus make erroneous decisions. The principle of "garbage in, garbage out" applies. However, a good manager does not block the flow of information and is constantly searching for the missing pieces that make the puzzle more complete.

Good managers are flexible. However, people who are constantly operating from their Adult ego states have overly strong ego state boundaries around the Adult. Consequently, their energy does not flow easily through their personalities, and they are unable to draw on all of their resources. As a consequence, they sometimes appear to be impersonal, much like a machine.

On the other end of this continuum are people who have weak Adult ego state boundaries, which gives them contaminated opinions and feelings. As a consequence, they are likely to be overdominated by their Child and Parent ego states. Such people are often tired physically and emotionally because the Adult does not assert the strength to control the Parent-Child inner dialogue. Thus this dialogue can serve as a continuous energy drain.

The Adult must gain strength in the personality without becoming rigid if it is to be a good manager. Just as a muscle strengthens with use and atrophies with disuse, a person can develop the Adult as manager of the personality by becoming aware of it, using it, and not fearing the responsibility that goes with the job.

EXERCISE 9. YOUR ADULT EGO STATE AT WORK

For many people, the Adult ego state is the one they use most often on the job. However, if they have authority over others, they may be acting more parental than they are aware of. If they have little or no authority, they may feel and act more childlike.

Think of a decision you recently made at work. How was each of your ego states involved?

- Adult logical thinking?

- Parental traditions?

- Child feelings?

Which ego state seemed to be most influential at the time? _____

As you think about it now, if you could do it over, would you choose to use more or less of any of your ego states? If so, in what ways?

The Adult Can Be Integrated

One goal of TA is to integrate the personality so that the Adult is not functioning merely like a mechanistic computer or like an under- or overdeveloped muscle. Rather, the goal is to release the Adult's capacity for directing the personality in such a way that it can call on the emotionally healthy parts of the Child and the emotionally healthy parts of the Parent ego states when appropriate.

As people's personalities become more integrated, they filter more and more Parent and Child material through their Adults. They expand their repertoires of possible behavior through learning. Berne writes:

> The mechanism of this "integration" remains to be elucidated, but it can be observed that certain people when functioning *qua* Adult have a charm and openness of nature which is reminiscent of that exhibited by children. Along with these go certain responsible feelings toward the rest of humanity which may be subsumed under the classical term "pathos." On the other hand, there are moral qualities which are universally expected of people who undertake grown-up responsibilities, such attributes as courage, sincerity, loyalty, and reliability, and which meet not mere local prejudices, but a world-wide ethos. In this sense the Adult can be said to have child-like and ethical aspects. . . . [6]
>
> . . . Transactionally, this means that anyone functioning as an [integrated] Adult should ideally exhibit three kinds of tendencies: personal attractivenss and responsiveness, objective data-processing, and ethical responsibility. . . . [7]

EXERCISE 10. ARE YOU INTEGRATING?

Recall a problem calling for social action around a health care issue to which you did or did not respond. Which ego states did you use in making your decision?

- Did you evaluate the opinions of your Parent ego state with your Adult and allow the OK nurturing ones to affect your actions? If so, how and in what ways?

- Did you evaluate the feelings and adaptions of your Child ego state with your Adult and allow the empathic feelings to affect your actions? If so, how and in what ways?

Would you consider your response an integrated one? If not, what part of you made the decision?

EXERCISE 11. EGO STATES IN THE PATIENT

Patients have ego states that can be energized. For example, a patient may easily be thrown into the Child ego state—may be scared and panicky, insecure and anxious, or rebellious and angry.

Describe ways in which a health care professional might unwittingly encourage a patient to be in the Child:

What are the consequences of the patient's being stuck in the Child

- for the staff?

- for the patient?

Describe ways in which a health care professional might encourage a patient to be in the Adult:

What are the consequences of the patient's being in the Adult

- for the staff?

- for the patient?

Describe ways in which a health care professional might encourage a patient to be in the Parent:

What are the consequences of the patient's being in the Parent

- for the staff?

- for the patient?

EXERCISE 12. IMPACT OF LABELS

Discuss the differences in ego state implication of referring to a person coming for health care services as a:

- Patient

- Client

- Customer

What are the advantages or disadvantages for each?

SUMMARY

Each person has three ego states—Parent, Adult, and Child. Each ego state has value and is necessary for forming a whole personality that is caring, intelligent, and joyful. Each ego state is active in giving and receiving health care.

All people have their parent figures in their heads. The imprints of these parent figures form the Parent ego state. At times a person acts, speaks, gestures, and thinks as his or her parent figures did. At other times, a person is influenced by the inner messages from those parent figures.

Every child is born with inherited characteristics; born into a specific social, economic, and emotional environment; and trained in certain ways by authority figures. Every child experiences significant events such as illness, pain, accidents, geographical dislocation, economic crisis, and death in the family. These influences contribute to the uniqueness of childhood for each person and form the Child ego state.

Every person also has an Adult ego state which, when used, deals with current reality. The Adult ego state is influenced by education and experience, but is not related to age. When it is activated, a person's Adult can collect and organize information, predict possible consequences of various actions, make conscious choices, and gain more control over communication patterns. Even though a choice is made from the Adult, it is not necessarily accurate if information is wrong or lacking. However, Adult awareness gives people more options over what they choose to do and serves to minimize regrettable actions, thus increasing a person's potential for even more successful healing practices.

UNIT 3
THE TRANSACTIONS PEOPLE USE

Have you worked with people who:

- seem to be on your same wavelength?

- often shut off the conversation?

- don't talk directly—they say one thing but mean another?

If so, you have observed the three basic types of transactions that occur whenever two or more people are together. These transactions are complementary, crossed, and ulterior.

HEALTH CARE TRANSACTIONS

Anything that happens between people involves a stimulus and a response. These are interpersonal *transactions* and occur between one or more ego states of one person and one or more ego states of another.

For example, sometimes a stimulus is sent from the Child in one person to the Child in another: "Hey, want to go to a party tonight?" Sometimes it is from the Adult in one to the Adult in another: "Have you read anything recently about burn treatment?" Sometimes the stimulus is from the Child in one to the Parent in another: "The muscles in my shoulder really hurt. How about a session with your magic fingers?" And at other times it's Parent to Child: "Just relax and open your mouth really wide for me. This isn't going to last very long." And at still other times the transaction is Parent to Parent: "I think its disgusting how sloppy the young people today are. Don't you?"

Of course, the responder has the option to choose which ego state to use. Many responses are impulsive and done without knowledge or thinking. The more awareness people have of their options, the more productive their transactions. Understanding typical kinds of transactions is a valuable tool for improving communications in health care and developing human resources. [1]

SOME TRANSACTIONS ARE COMPLEMENTARY

A complementary transaction occurs when a message sent from one ego state gets the expected response from a specific ego state in the other person. In this case the lines of communication are open. For example:

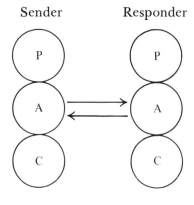

Sender   Responder

1. "Do you know where the emergency oxygen is kept?"
2. "It is in the storeroom next to the emergency room staff entrance."

The same initial question can be asked with such different gestures, facial expressions, and tone of voice that it elicits a different response. For example, a stimulus originating in one person's Child ego state frequently brings out the Parent ego state in another:

Sender   Responder

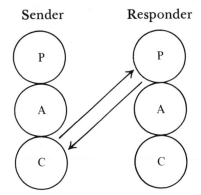

1. (With a worried look) "Do you know where the emergency oxygen supply is kept?"
2. (In a nurturing sympathetic voice) "Don't fret. The respiratory therapist is getting it now."

Or, it may activate the Child in another:

Sender   Responder

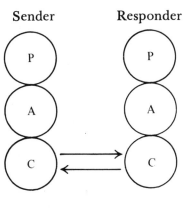

1. (Angrily kicking the leg of the desk) "Where is the darned oxygen supply?"
2. "Isn't this place a zoo! You can never get what you want around here."

Sometimes a complementary transaction can be from one Parent ego state to another:

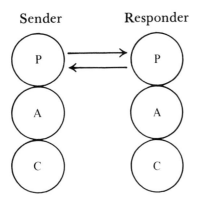

1. "I feel so sorry that little Jim has to be on IVs and gastric suction oxygen."
2. "I do, too. He looks so uncomfortable and forlorn."

To more fully understand any communication, one needs to consider the nonverbal aspects as well as the spoken words. All nonverbal aspects contribute to the *meaning* in every transaction. Understanding another person's meaning usually clarifies communication and enhances relationships.

EXERCISE 1. ANALYZING COMPLEMENTARY TRANSACTIONS

Develop dialogue commonly used in health care situations that fits the following diagrams. If necessary for clarification, include tone of voice, facial expression, etc. Use illustrations from your job setting.

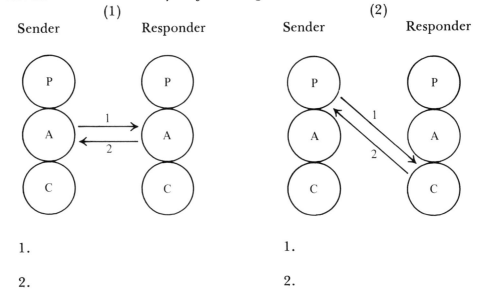

(1)

1.

2.

(2)

1.

2.

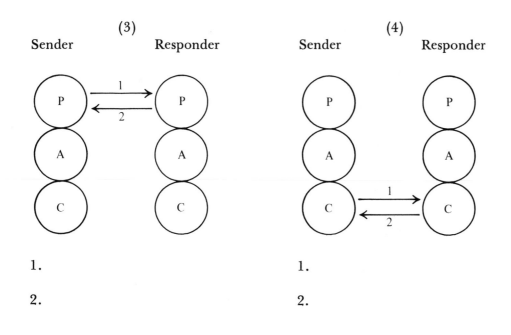

1.

2.

1.

2.

SOME TRANSACTIONS ARE CROSSED

When two people stand glaring at each other, turn their backs on each other, are unwilling to continue transacting, or are puzzled by what has just occurred between them, it is likely that they have just experienced a *crossed transaction.* Crossed transactions are a frequent source of resentment between people. For example:

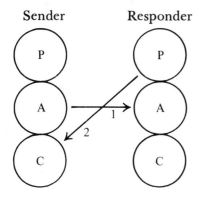

1.   "Here is Mr. Jones's medical report."
2.   "Does it always take you this long?"

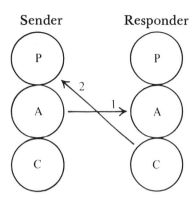

1.   "Do you know where the medication orders are?"
2.   "Don't ask me. I never saw that chart."

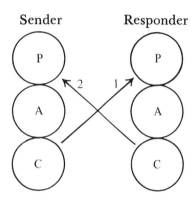

1.   "Please help me 'prep' this patient. I'm getting so tired."
2.   "Boy, you think you're tired! I had to work the late shift last night."

Crossed transactions occur whenever an unexpected response is made to the stimulus. An ego state is activated unexpectedly, and communication between the people is closed off. At this point, people tend to withdraw, turn away from each other, or switch the conversation in another direction. Crossed transactions often happen in already tense moments such as the urgency of a life-threatening situation in which patient care is critical and anxiety runs high. Such tension can actually block hearing and distort what people really intend.

Although crossed transactions often close off communication lines and turn people away from each other, sometimes they are useful. They may stop or shorten an unwanted or unproductive conversation or stop a psychological game. (Games are discussed in Unit 5.)

EXERCISE 2. ANALYZING CROSSED TRANSACTIONS

Develop dialogue from your work experience that fits the following diagrams. Include the behavior if it clarifies the transaction.

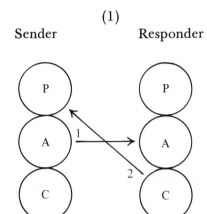

(1)

Sender   Responder

1.

2.

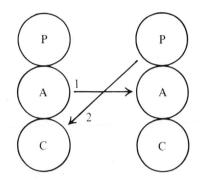

(2)

Sender   Responder

1.

2.

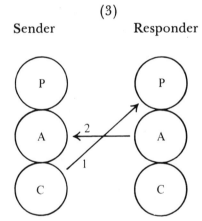

(3)

Sender   Responder

1.

2.

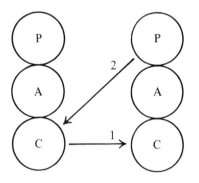

(4)

Sender   Responder

1.

2.

How effective are each of the transactions above?

- Do they facilitate staff communication? _____

- Do they facilitate patient care? _____

If not effective, what could be changed?

SOME TRANSACTIONS HAVE ULTERIOR MESSAGES

An ulterior message can occur anywhere people communicate. At the social level is the plausible, surface message, but underneath is the ulterior, or psychological, message, which has a different agenda. The ulterior, or psychological, message is usually what the communication is really about. It often involves a "come-on," a "put-off," or a "put-down."

If a physician says to a group of nurses: "Here is our latest research on childbirth, but it may not interest you," the physician is sending a message to them that may elicit anger. On the social level, information is offered. At the psychological level, a put-down is implied. This put-down, thinly disguised, is the ulterior motive. Ulterior transactions are diagrammed with a solid line for the social level and a dotted line for the psychological level. The psychological level is often nonverbal.

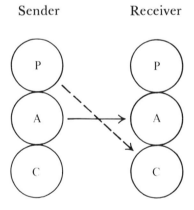

Another ulterior message could be given by a lab technician who turns in an incomplete report, thus inviting the Parent in the doctor or nurse to make a critical remark. A physician who is continually late with appointments or a nurse who frequently fails to have charts ready may also be inviting a Parent put-down. Such invitations are usually done outside of awareness and are often justified with a strong sense of "rightness."

Sender   Receiver

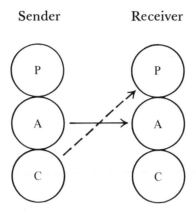

A particular kind of ulterior transaction is colloquially called the "gallows transaction." [2] This occurs when one makes jokes and laughs about one's self-destructive behavior. In essence, the laugh says, "Don't take me and what I say seriously." It also invites the listener to laugh in response, thus confirming that the person making the joke is in fact not to be treated seriously. For example, a young man brought into emergency with multiple cuts might laughingly phone his friends and say, "I just smashed up my car again." In other words, while he is telling about self-defeating behavior, he smiles as if it is clever. He thus reinforces the Child to keep himself in trouble. The laughing response from his friends also reinforces his self-defeating behavior, "tightening the noose."

The real issue is thus avoided. Nobody says, "Why are you laughing? It's not funny." Such a confrontation shows a refusal to go along with the self-destructive pattern.

It's often an invitation to a gallows transaction when people say such things as: "I fell off my diet again. (ha, ha)" "As usual, I forgot to take my medication. (ha, ha)" "My kid's the most accident-prone kid on the block. (ha, ha)" "This time I nearly knocked out all of her teeth. (ha, ha)" "Boy, you should have seen me last night. I really tied one on. (ha, ha)"

EXERCISE 3. ANALYZING ULTERIOR TRANSACTIONS

Try your hand at indentifying the social and psychological levels of the following transaction.

Stimulus
"Sorry this is late. I know you needed it this morning." (Sighs, meaning, "Kick me, I'm bad.")

Response
"It's too late to be used." (Frowns, meaning, "OK, here's your kick.")

Now diagram the social transaction with solid lines and the ulterior transaction with broken lines.

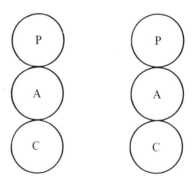

Now discuss and diagram a gallows transaction you've observed at work.

EXERCISE 4. PERFORMANCE AND ULTERIOR TRANSACTIONS

Discuss at least two typical ulterior transactions that occur in your work setting.

What happens as a result of these kinds of transactions:

- To productivity?

- To morale?

- To excellence in patient care?

EXERCISE 5. TRANSACTIONAL RESPONSES

Design possible ego state *responses* to these various stimuli.

Stimulus: A co-worker comes to work blurry-eyed and tired.

Possible Responses:

- Parent

- Adult

- Child

Which of the transactions above are complementary? Which are crossed? Which are ulterior?

Stimulus: When a deadline is given that is extremely demanding and difficult to meet.

Possible Responses:

• Parent

• Adult

• Child

Which of the transactions above are complementary? Which are crossed? Which are ulterior?

Stimulus: Attention is called to a bad error.

Possible Responses:

• Parent

• Adult

• Child

Which of the transactions above are complementary? Which are crossed? Which are ulterior?

Communication Analysis: Now work in small groups to identify important communication problems and situations in your particular organization. Then develop possible Parent, Adult, and Child responses to each of these situations.

Situation

Possible ego state responses

P

A

C

Which of these responses would work the best?

EXERCISE 6. CHOOSING YOUR RESPONSES

In this exercise check the response that is nearest to the way you would react. Work quickly, giving your *intuitive* response.

Situation 1

You are planning a new administrative change, but the planning is not yet complete. A co-worker, speaking from the Parent ego state, asks, "What's going on here?" You would:

_____ 1. Tell him all about it.

_____ 2. Ask him why he wants to know.

_____ 3. Change the subject.

_____ 4. Tell him you're thinking of making a change, but have not completed your plans.

———— 5. Wink or give him a sly look.

———— 6. (Other) ————————————————————

Situation 2

Your superior issues instructions loudly while frowning and banging on his desk, just as his father used to do. The instructions, if followed, will result in serious financial loss. You would:

———— 1. Do what he says and not say anything.

———— 2. Tell him he's wrong, but you'll do it.

———— 3. Do what he says and tell others about his error in judgment.

———— 4. Explain why the loss will result.

———— 5. Argue with him.

———— 6. (Other) ————————————————————

Situation 3

Someone with less seniority and who frequently fools around gets the promotion you were working for. You would.

———— 1. Talk to the boss about it.

———— 2. Complain to your other co-workers.

———— 3. Feel depressed, but stay silent.

———— 4. Be angry about it and take out your anger on someone else.

———— 5. Start to avoid the person who gets the promotion.

———— 6. (Other) ————————————————————

Situation 4

You have an important date for the evening. Then someone on your staff takes off with an unexpected illness. There is no alternative but to stay late. You would:

———— 1. Object strongly and refuse to do it.

———— 2. Object strongly, then say you'll do it.

_____ 3. Comply silently.

_____ 4. Feel sorry for yourself and look downcast.

_____ 5. Cancel your date because you were "glad to help out."

_____ 6. (Other) _____

Now look back at the responses you checked. How many of your responses were complementary? Crossed? Ulterior? Are you satisfied with your choices? Why or why not?

EXERCISE 7. COMMUNICATION ANALYSIS IN TRIADS

This exercise will take twenty-five to thirty minutes. To do it you will need three people or groups of three to form triads. Each person will take a turn being speaker, listener, and analyzer in the small groups.

The subject to be discussed is: "One of the biggest communication problems in our organization is. . . ."

The roles of the triads are as follows:

- Speaker will talk about the subject as he or she perceives it.

- Listener will listen to what the speaker is saying and be actively involved in trying to understand. The listener will ask questions for clarification and draw the speaker out by giving feedback.

- Analyzer will observe and keep track of some of the complementary, crossed, and ulterior transactions and give feedback to the other two group members.

- After seven to ten minutes, the triads will switch. The speaker will become the analyzer, the listener will become the speaker, and the analyzer will become the listener. The same subject or a different one will then be discussed, following the same process.

- After seven to ten minutes, switch roles once more, so that each person in the triad has had a chance to play each of three parts.

HUMAN RIGHTS IMPACT TRANSACTIONS

To be human is to be connected and to transact with other persons. To be human is to have rights. People who do not have rights (as in some institutions) are dehumanized. When this happens, they are treated as objects instead of as persons.

The recognition of human rights is related to the quality of transactions. Crossed and ulterior transactions from a superiority position often indicate "you are not-OK and therefore do not have the same rights as I have." Crossed and ulterior transactions from an anxious or hopeless position often indicate "I am not-OK and therefore am not entitled to as many rights as you."

In health care settings that are healthy, both providers and recipients have rights.

The American Hospital Association presents a Patient's Bill of Rights with the expectation that observance of these rights will contribute to more effective patient care and greater satisfaction for the patient, his physician, and the hospital organization. Further, the Association presents these rights in the expectation that they will be supported by the hospital on behalf of its patients, as an integral part of the healing process. It is recognized that a personal relationship between the physician and the patient is essential for the provision of proper medical care. The traditional physician-patient relationship takes on a new dimension when care is rendered within an organizational structure. Legal precedent has established that the institution itself also has a responsibility to the patient. It is in recognition of these factors that these rights are affirmed.

1.   The patient has the right to considerate and respectful care.

2.   The patient has the right to obtain from his physician complete current information concerning his diagnosis, treatment, and prognosis in terms the patient can be reasonably expected to understand. When it is not medically advisable to give such information to the patient, the information should be made available to an appropriate person in his behalf. He has the right to know, by name, the physician responsible for coordinating his care.

3.   The patient has the right to receive from his physician information necessary to give informed consent prior to the start of any procedure and/or treatment. Except in emergencies, such information for informed consent should include but not necessarily be limited to the specific procedure and/or treatment, the medically significant risks involved, and the probable duration of incapacitation. Where medically significant alternatives for care or treatment exist, or when the patient requests information concerning medical alternatives, the patient has the right to such information. The patient also has the right to know the name of the person responsible for the procedures and/or treatment.

4.   The patient has the right to refuse treatment to the extent permitted by law and to be informed of the medical consequences of his action.

5.   The patient has the right to every consideration of his privacy concerning his own medical care program. Case discussion, consultation, examination, and treatment are confidential and should be conducted discreetly. Those not directly involved in his care must have the permission of the patient to be present.

6.   The patient has the right to expect that all communications and records pertaining to his care should be treated as confidential.

7.   The patient has the right to expect that within its capacity a hospital must make reasonable response to the request of a patient for services. The hospital must provide evaluation, service, and/or referral as indicated by the urgency of the case. When medically permissible, a patient may be transferred to another facility only after he has received complete information and explanation concerning the needs for and alternatives to such a transfer. The institution to which the patient is to be transferred must first have accepted the patient for transfer.

8.   The patient has the right to obtain information as to any relationship of his hospital to other health care and educational institutions insofar as his care is concerned. The patient has the right to obtain information as to the existence of any professional relationships among individuals, by name, who are treating him.

9.   The patient has the right to be advised if the hospital proposes to engage in or perform human experimentation affecting his care or treatment. The patient has the right to refuse to participate in such research projects.

10.   The patient has the right to expect reasonable continuity of care. He has the right to know in advance what appointment times and physicians are available and where. The patient has the right to expect that the hospital will provide a mechanism whereby he is informed by his physician or a delegate of the physician of the patient's continuing health care requirements following discharge.

11.   The patient has the right to examine and receive an explanation of his bill regardless of source of payment.

12.   The patient has the right to know what hospital rules and regulations apply to his conduct as a patient.

No catalog of rights can guarantee for the patient the kind of treatment he has a right to expect. A hospital has many functions to perform, including the prevention and treatment of disease, the education of both health professionals and patients, and the conduct of clinical research. All these activities must be conducted with an overriding concern for the patient, and, above all, the recognition of his dignity as a human being. Success in achieving this recognition assures success in the defense of the rights of the patient.*

*Reprinted with the permission of the American Hospital Association, Copyright 1975.

EXERCISE 8. HUMAN RIGHTS OF HEALTH CARE PROVIDERS

Not only do patients have rights, but so too do health care providers. Some of these rights are specified by law or a policy manual. Others are less clear.

Discuss and then write out a reasonable Bill of Rights for your job situation, using the following format.

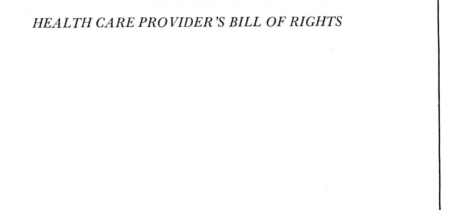

HEALTH CARE PROVIDER'S BILL OF RIGHTS

Now go back over the Health Care Provider's Bill of Rights and discuss how these rights would change the transactions on the job between staff and patient, among staff, between administration and line staff, etc. Make your answers as concrete and as picturable as possible.

SUMMARY

In interpersonal relations the unit of measure is the transaction. By analyzing transactions people can gain a conscious control of how they operate with others. They can determine when transactions are complementary, crossed, or ulterior. Understanding these three basic ways of communicating can assist you in expanding winning ways with staff and clients.

In healthy relationships people transact directly, straightforwardly, and, on occasion, intensely. These transactions tend to be complementary and free from ulterior motives. Healthy ways of transacting help to create healthier people and healthier work environments.

Ideally, when communication lines between people are improved and strengthened, the systems all work more positively to facilitate the goals of the organization. Patients get better faster, time (and money) that would otherwise be used in salvaging miscommunications are saved, and people feel better about the successes they've had on their jobs.

UNIT 4

STROKES AND PSYCHOLOGICAL TRADING STAMPS

Have you ever worked with people who:

- hold resentments and then blow up at the slightest provocation?

- reject compliments?

- show appreciation and are a pleasure to be around?

If you have, you have observed people giving, receiving, and rejecting positive or negative strokes. A stroke is any form of touch or recognition—"any act implying recognition of another's presence." [1] It is part of a transaction. For example, "How are you feeling today?" "Much better, thank you" is a two-stroke transaction.

Every person has the need to be touched and to be recognized by other people—to have his or her existence validated. These are biological and phychological needs which can be thought of as "hungers." The hungers for touch and recognition are appeased with strokes. These strokes can be positive or negative and are usually given in the form of actual physical touch or by some symbolic form of recognition, such as a look, a word, a gesture, or any act that says "I know you're there."

PEOPLE NEED STROKES TO SURVIVE

Infants will not grow normally without the touch of others. Something about being touched stimulates their chemistry for mental and physical growth. Among transactional analysts there is a saying: "If the infant is not stroked, his spinal cord shrivels up." [2] Infants who are neglected, ignored, or for any reason do not experience enough touch suffer mental and physical deterioration, even to the point of death.

The documentary film *Second Chance,* which is summarized below, dramatically illustrates this need. [3]

When Susan's father left her at a large children's hospital, she was 22 months old. However, she weighed only 15 pounds (the weight of a five-month-old baby) and was 28 inches tall (the average height of a ten-month-old). She had practically no motor skills, could not crawl, could not speak or even babble. If people approached her, she withdrew in tears.

After three weeks during which no one had come to see Susan, a social worker contacted the mother. Both mother and father were above average in education, yet the mother complained, "Babies are a poor excuse for human beings." She described Susan as not liking to be held and wanting to be left alone. She said she had given up trying to make contact with Susan and, in regard to taking care of her, admitted, "I don't want to do that anymore."

Examinations showed no physical reason for Susan's extreme mental and physical retardation, and her case was diagnosed as "maternal deprivation syndrome."

A volunteer substitute mother was called in to give Susan loving care for six hours a day, five days a week. The hospital staff also gave Susan much attention, and she was held, rocked, played with, and fed with an abundance of physical touching.

Two months later, although she was still markedly retarded, Susan had a highly developed affectional response. She had also gained six pounds and had grown two inches. Her motor ability was greatly improved. She could crawl and could walk if holding on. Without fear she could relate to relative strangers. Tender loving care had had a remarkable effect on Susan. [4]

As a child grows older, the early primary hunger for actual physical touch is modified and becomes hunger for recognition. A smile, a nod, a word, a frown, a gesture begin to substitute for some touch strokes. Like touch, these forms of recognition, whether positive or negative, stimulate the brain of the one receiving them and serve to verify the fact that the person is there and alive. Recognition strokes also keep the nervous system from "shriveling."

Although either negative or positive strokes may stimulate an infant's body chemistry, it takes *positive strokes* to develop emotionally healthy persons with a sense of OKness. The lack of sufficient strokes tends to have a detrimental effect on people, no strokes being the worst of all.

Positive strokes range in value from the minimal maintenance of a "hello" to the depth encounter of intimacy. If the stroking is authentic, honestly jibes with the facts, and is not overdone, it nourishes a person. In such a case the person receiving the strokes collects a "good" feeling (a gold stamp).

Positive strokes encourage a person to feel good, alive, alert, and significant. At a greater depth they enhance one's sense of well-being, endorse intelligence, and are often pleasurable. The feelings beneath positive strokes are feelings of good will and convey the I'm OK and You're OK position. Good strokes create a positive energy that stimulates productivity.

Stroke hunger is often felt on the job. [5] In one laboratory a supervisor complained that one of her lab workers was spending too much time at the water cooler, leaving his isolated lab every hour looking for someone to talk to. The supervisor, after being trained in TA, [6] made it a practice to poke her head in the lab at intervals for a brief but friendly chat with this worker. The trips into the hallway diminished considerably, and in the long run these moments of contact saved time. As this supervisor discovered, there are varying needs for recognition.

Patients too need strokes. Even pain intensity might be related to strokes. Not uncommonly patients receive more medication for pain at night. There

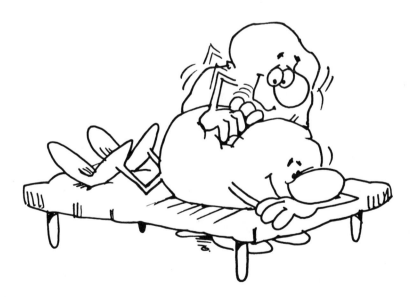

appears to be no physiological evidence that pain is more intense at night. Perhaps the increased sense of intensity is more related to aloneness and loneliness. In fact, even in less serious situations, some patients might call a nurse for service just to keep their "spinal columns from shriveling up." It's important to healing that these needs are met. People are more and more realizing the importance of touch to promote health. [7]

STROKES APPEAL TO DIFFERENT EGO STATES

As people transact, they are continually stroking different ego states in one another. Strokes for behavior, such as being fun, following orders, not interrupting, staying clean, and being creative, are likely felt by the Child. Strokes for such things as following tradition, setting limits, nurturing others, and being a good cook may be felt by the Parent. Strokes for competence, accuracy, and computation may be felt by the Adult.

However, people differ from one another. Each ego state in each person may want different kinds of strokes. Since each person's ego states are different, each person's Parent, Adult, and Child accepts and looks for different strokes. [8] A positive stroke to one person may seem negative to another. Sometimes what is "assumed" may or may not be true. For example, women traditionally have been assumed to value strokes for appearance (Child) over strokes for competence (Adult), whereas the opposite is often assumed true of men. As a result, some women complain of lack of acceptance as intelligent, capable people, whereas men, deprived of strokes for the Child, may feel unappreciated or even unloved. [9]

EXERCISE 1. COMMON STROKES IN HEALTH CARE

What kinds of strokes in a typical health care environment have you observed that are *positive* and *nourishing?*

- Between nurses

- Between professional and nonprofessional staff

- Between staff and patients

- Between doctors and nurses

What kinds of strokes in a typical health care environment have you observed that are *negative* and *noxious?*

- Between nurses

- Between professional and nonprofessional staff

- Between staff and patients

- Between doctors and nurses

Where and when in health care situations have you observed an absence of strokes when strokes would be helpful?

- Between nurses

- Between professional and nonprofessional staff

- Between staff and patients

- Between doctors and nurses

Now focus on the kinds of strokes patients receive.

- Do they get more strokes for health or illness?

- Are the strokes they receive geared to promoting healing?

- Do patients' needs or organizational needs get more strokes?

EXERCISE 2. THE STROKES YOU GET

Recall a recent stroke you received that you felt at an intense level.

- What was said or done?

- How did you feel?

- What did you do?

- Are you satisfied with this?

- If not, what would you have liked to have done?

Recall a person whose strokes are important to you.

- What kind of stroke do you like to receive from that person?

- What kind do you try to avoid from that person?

- What kind of stroke do you want more of from that person?

EXERCISE 3. THE STROKES YOU GIVE

How do you usually stroke patients in each of the following circumstances:

- What do you usually do or say?

In chronic illness	In acute illness or accident	In terminal illness

- How do patients tend to respond?

In chronic illness	In acute illness or accident	In terminal illness

- What are the health-promoting qualities of your strokes?

In chronic illness	*In acute illness or accident*	*In terminal illness*

How do you usually stroke the people with whom you work in the following situations:

- What do you usually do and say?

In a staff meeting	*In routine, daily work*	*In a critical situation*

- How do others tend to respond?

In a staff meeting	*In routine, daily work*	*In a critical situation*

- How does what you do affect patient care?

In a staff meeting	*In routine, daily work*	*In a critical situation*

PEOPLE COLLECT GOOD AND BAD FEELINGS

Collecting a good feeling from a positive stroke is collecting a "gold stamp." Collecting a bad feeling from a negative stroke is collecting a "gray stamp." In transactional analysis the good or bad feelings a person collects are called psychological "trading stamps." The term "stamps" is borrowed from the practice in some parts of the country of collecting trading stamps when making purchases and later redeeming them for merchandise. [10] People tend to follow a similar practice with their feelings.

A specific color is sometimes assigned a stamp to represent a bad feeling: red stamps for anger, blue stamps for hurt feelings and depression, white stamps for purity and self-righteousness, green stamps for jealousy and envy, etc. Perhaps at times you've felt red with rage or green with envy.

The color assigned to psychological trading stamps is, of course, unimportant. The important point is the fact that psychological trading stamps represent an indulgence in bad feelings learned in childhood which are sought after, saved up, and eventually "redeemed."

PREFERRED COLLECTIONS START IN CHILDHOOD

Children are not born with all of their feelings already programmed toward objects and people. They learn toward whom and toward what they can show affection. They learn toward whom and about what to feel guilty. They learn whom and what to fear and hate. In effect, they learn how to give and to receive certain kinds of strokes. Although each child experiences all feelings, each eventually adapts with a learned feeling that becomes preferred as a "favored" feeling. This is often what was *commonly* felt when things "got tough" around the house.

A child who continually hears "I'm ashamed of you!" or "You should be ashamed of yourself!" learns to collect guilt feelings.

A child who continually hears "Just wait until your father gets home; he'll beat you good!" learns to collect fear.

A child who continually hears "Don't speak to those people; they can't be trusted" learns to collect anger or suspicion stamps.

A child who continually hears "What's the matter with you! Can't you do anything right!" learns to collect stupid or inadequacy stamps.

These feelings may have been an understandable response to the original childhood situations. However, problems arise when later in life people tend to seek out situations in which they get a particular stroke so that they can *re-experience the same old feelings.* These feelings become their negative stamp collections and feel "right" to them because of their childhood experiences. It's what they know.

Most people know someone whose low self-opinion motivates him or her to act way below potential. For example, people who in childhood took the position "I'm stupid" later do stupid things so that others once more call them "stupid." Sometimes stupid actions cause others pain or inconvenience, but at a more serious level they can be life-or-death matters. For example, Donnelly didn't learn to use math in school and was called "Dummy." On the job Donnelly frequently felt frustrated and unable to calculate a fractional dose of medication, so was called "Dummy" again by the supervisor—just like parents and teachers used to do.

If people want to add to their collection of negative feelings, they manipulate others to hurt them, to belittle them, to anger them, to frighten them, or to arouse their guilt. They accomplish this by provoking or inviting others to play certain roles.

Some go a step further and *imagine* that another person has done something negative to them. They thus collect a *counterfeit* feeling. For example, a patient might imagine, "I knew that nursing assistant didn't like me by the way he looked at me," when actually the assistant was frowning because of being worried about a home problem.

Sometimes a flurry of being "too busy" leads people into passing out an abundance of gray stamps and few gold ones. This can become part of the system's script. As one nurse pointed out, "Health care systems are not set up for praise. Something else always comes first. 'A job well done,' would be music to my ears!"

EXERCISE 4. YOUR NEGATIVE STAMP COLLECTION

Recall a situation in the last week in which you collected a negative feeling.

• What was the situation?

• Who was involved?

• What feeling(s) did you collect?

• What did you "do" with your feelings? Are you holding them, or did you cash them in?

• Could you have handled the situation differently so that you didn't collect?

• Is your pattern in any way similar to one of your parent figures or the way you acted when you were little?

COLLECTING GOOD FEELINGS IS SUPPORTIVE

When people collect good feelings from positive strokes, they collect a warm emotion—warm "fuzzies." When people collect bad feelings from negative strokes, they collect cold responses—cold "pricklies." [11]

Stroke collections accumulate throughout a person's lifetime and help shape one's attitude and approach to most of life's activities. When there is a temporary, drastic, or sudden change in one's physical, social, or emotional well-being, a reserve stroke collection may help or hinder a person's response. An accumulation of warm fuzzies fosters hope. An accumulation of cold pricklies fosters despair. In response to the same "bad news" after a physical examination, two patients demonstrated a dramatic difference. While one was bemoaning, "I'll never get over this," the other was saying, "This is one of the toughest things I've ever faced, but I know I'll make it."

In health care settings feelings are collected by staff as well as by patients. In hospitals, for example, housekeepers who do not feel appreciated by other staff members, nurses who feel put upon by doctors' requests, or doctors who feel put down by administrators often collect bad feelings. These collections create an unhealthy work environment. In contrast, words of appreciation and acts of respect lead to collections of positive feelings, which in turn create a healthy climate. These positive feelings help to direct people's energies toward constructive behavior that stimulates positive action and lightens the load.

STAMPS ARE EVENTUALLY CASHED IN

People eventually cash in their bad feelings—sometimes in bunches and sometimes a few at a time. Have you ever seen a put down collected and passed down a chain of command? For example, one head of cardiology received a negative stroke from a spouse before leaving for work in the morning. No resolution of the problem was made. So the bad feelings were collected and carried off to work. At work they were cashed in on one of the nurse supervisors: "What's the matter with you? I expected this record at 6 A.M., not 8 A.M.!" The supervisor collected bad feelings and took them back to the record-delivery person to cash in: "Didn't you see the request I left? Why can't you get things to me on time? I also found several alphabetical errors." The delivery person went home and cashed in on a spouse: "Why haven't you finished that painting job? The place looks a mess— as usual!" The spouse turned to the children: "You can't do anything right. Look at the stuff you've left around for all of us to stumble over!"And the children cashed in by kicking the dog!

People acquire collections of different sizes and have different compulsions as to when, where, and how to redeem their negative collections. Some people collect the equivalent of a page of stamps and turn them in for relatively small prizes: having a headache, throwing a pencil, dropping a thermometer, bawling out an assistant, spilling a file drawer, or mailing a bill in the wrong envelope.

For some people, however, the prize is somewhat bigger. If they have saved several "books" of gray stamps, they then feel justified when they do such things as wreck an important piece of equipment; injure themselves; quit school, job, treatment, or an important relationship; take drugs from the locked cupboard; fire a valued employee; pull the wrong tooth, foul up the shift change; and so forth.

Occasionally people save an even larger collection, cashing it in for a larger prize: a mental breakdown, imprisonment, dropping out of society, injuring someone, or losing a valued career. The "biggest" game players, "go for the kill"— suicide or homicide.

When people feel that they have collected enough stamps and are ready to cash them in, certain words and phrases are often used to indicate that redemption time is close at hand. Have you ever heard (or said):

That's the last straw!

I've taken all I'm going to!

I've had it up to here!

I'm sorry, but . . .

Dear John . . .

EXERCISE 5. CASHING IN NEGATIVE STAMPS

What are other possible words, phrases, body messages that could indicate that a pile of resentment is about to be redeemed? Develop at least two.

Look back at the feelings you collected in Exercise 4. If you cashed them in, how did you do it? What was your "prize"?

Now discuss some typical ways you see "cash-ins" happening in your organization. (For example, "slowdowns" are often subtle ways of expressing rebellion.)

In contrast to cashing in bad feelings, people can collect enough good feelings about themselves so that they feel justified in doing something good for themselves. They may "cash in" their gold stamps by decorating the office, buying themselves flowers, having a fun weekend, getting a massage, listening to their favorite music, ringing up a special friend, or taking a pleasant vacation. Again, the size of the collection usually determines the size of the prize.

When cashing in gold stamps, people need to be aware of the possible temptation to collect some old gray stamps. For example, if a person is on a weight-loss program, cashing in for drinks and a big spaghetti and spumoni dinner could eventually result in a collection of bad feelings.

EXERCISE 6. YOUR GOLD STAMP COLLECTION

Recall at least two situations during the past two weeks in which you received positive strokes and collected gold stamps.

- What was the situation?

- Who was involved?

- How did you feel?

- Does the memory of it make you feel good now?

What good things do you do for yourself when you *cash in* gold stamps?

Over the next week attempt to be conscious of your collections of good and bad feelings. Make your gold stamp collection larger. Diminish your negative stamp collection.

EXERCISE 7. ENLARGING THE GOLD STAMP COLLECTIONS

How does your organization take care of the staff's stroke needs now?

Discuss ways to *increase* the gold stamp collections:

- In your work group

- Between departments (or factions)

- Between doctors and nurses

- Between staff and patients

Discuss ways in which clients could be encouraged to give *positive* feedback as well as negative feedback regarding their experiences as health care recipients.

SUMMARY

Everyone needs strokes to survive and to maintain a sense of well-being. Environments that are void of good strokes are sterile and do not promote healing. Motivation and productivity among staff also go down.

Many feelings are adapted in childhood. A person may have learned to respond with a preferred negative feeling—such as fear, guilt, anger, hurt, inadequacy—when things went wrong in the family. Later this feeling is sought after without awareness. In fact, one of the reasons psychological games are played is to give and receive negative stamps.

People can collect psychological gray stamps—bad feelings—hold on to them, and then cash them in for an unpleasant prize. Good feelings about one's self — gold stamps—can also be collected and redeemed for a pleasant prize. With awareness, people can expand their taste for and repertoire of gold stamps.

Good strokes make the world a better place to be in. They promote cooperation, productivity, and healing.

UNIT 5

GAMES PEOPLE PLAY

Have you ever felt:

* that you get more than your share of criticism?

* like yelling at someone for having botched things up?

* rejected after trying to help someone?

If so, you have experienced the basic drama roles of Victim, Persecutor, and Rescuer. [1] These are the classic roles that fit into scripts and are acted out in psychological games.

In the psychological games people play, there are maneuvers similar to those in "fun" games such as monopoly, checkers, or poker. In both types of games the players must *know* the game in order to play, follow definite rules for each move, and be prepared for someone to lose. However, psychological games are not played for fun. In fact, such games nearly always end with one or both parties feeling not-OK. Both have given and received negative strokes, have collected and "cashed in" negative stamps.

GAMES ARE NEGATIVE TRANSACTIONS

Psychological games can be played anywhere there are people—hospitals, offices, clinics, convalescent homes, as well as in nonwork situations. Everyone plays games, but most are not aware of doing so. They unknowingly choose others who know the rules and will play the opposite roles.

Although there are many different games, each has at least three basic elements: (1) a series of complementary transactions, which on the surface seem plausible; (2) an ulterior transaction, which is the hidden agenda, or motive; and (3) a negative payoff of bad or self-righteous feelings, which concludes the game and is the real purpose for playing it. In short, a game starts with a move which is like a con, designed to appeal to a weakness in the other player, and moves toward a predictable conclusion. [2]

Games tend to be repetitive. They prevent honest, intimate, and open relationships between the players. People find themselves saying the same old words in the same old way; only the time and place may change. They may even say, "I feel as if I've been through all this before—I even vowed: 'I'm just not going to get into that same hassle again,'—then we're face to face and it happens!"

People play games with different degrees of intensity—from a socially accepted relaxed level, such as giving a "come-on" followed by a brushoff, to a more serious level, ending up in prison, the hospital, or the morgue. Characteristic of all games is that things do not get better when they are played. When things do not get better, problems are not being solved. The energy that goes into games is diverted. Yet people play games because the games reinforce their early opinions about themselves and others, provide a way of getting and giving strokes, structure time, and fulfill a sense of identity and destiny which is characteristic of psychological scripts. [3]

GAMES INVOLVE DRAMA ROLES

Games are like short scenes in a life drama. There may be an intermission between the games, yet like a drama, the actors choose their roles, and the show goes on.

Games involve the dramatic roles of Victim, Persecutor, and Rescuer—the roles learned in childhood that later become part of a person's act. (When capitalized, these refer to phony, play-acting roles—roles played with a vested interest—not to actual victims, rescuers, and persecutors.)

Games that start from a Persecutor or Rescuer role reinforce the Persecutor's negative attitude: "You're not-OK" (so you need to be punished or saved). Games played from the Victim role reinforce a negative position about oneself: "I'm not-OK" (I need you to punish me or rescue me or forgive me.).

Many people act as if they expect to be Victims. They may even ask others to scold them or criticize them. For example, in one popular weight-loss program the nurse in charge reports that many people plead: "Please bawl me out if I gain weight; maybe it will help me stop eating so much." Such direct requests come from people who feel like Victims inviting someone else to play the Persecutor role.

Drama roles can be diagrammed as follows: [4]

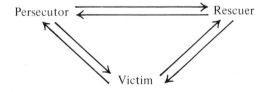

The dramatic action happens when the roles are switched.

Following are two examples:

- Ms. B (Victim):   I still feel tired most of the time.

  Dr. K (Rescuer):   Along with medication, you must get more exercise.

  Ms. B (Switching form Victim to Persecutor):   Yes, but you *told* me to take it easy and not overexert myself.

  Dr. K (Switching from Rescuer to Persecutor): Well, didn't you read the directions I sent home with you!

- Mr. R (Victim):   Doc, this shoulder is terrible. I can't stand the pain, so I get drunk every night.

  Dr. S (Rescuer):   Well now, Mr. R, you've been under a lot of stress. Take a few days off and just relax.

  Mr. R (Switching from Victim to Persecutor): Relax! Are you kidding! I've got three kids to support and now these doctor bills.

Even organizations sometimes act from Persecutor or Rescuer positions or are at least perceived that way by patients. One clinic reinforced this attitude with: "Please don't bother us with questions. We'll make the decisions." Then if something goes wrong, the patient may accuse: "Well, I let you make the decision; now look what's happened." (Now I've got you, you S.O.B.) Occasionally institutions intentionally do not conform to standards and are persecuted by a withdrawal of financial support, a negative utilization review, withdrawal of accreditation, or a malpractice suit. (*Kick Me*)

EXERCISE 1. ROLES IN THE TRIANGLE

List adjectives to describe typical on-the-job behavior of people when acting from each of the following roles:

Victim   *Persecutor*   *Rescuer*

List common phrases that a person might say when acting in each of the roles.

Victim   *Persecutor*   *Rescuer*

Discuss the roles palyed in your work situations between a patient and a health care provider:

- Who seems to play the Victim and in what situations? Does the Victim switch roles?

- Who plays the Rescuer and in what situations? Does the Rescuer switch roles?

- Who plays the Persecutor and in what situations? Does the the Persecutor switch roles?

    Because health care providers are often perceived as rescuers, discuss at least two examples that show the difference between a real rescuer and a phony Rescuer.

EACH GAME HAS A PLAN

Roles form the dramatic, repetitious actions characteristic of a psychological game. The ulterior purpose of a game is often revealed when the switch occurs and someone gets "caught in the act" or provokes a kick. Identifying the original roles and switch in roles serves to pinpoint a game interaction.

    Another useful way to identify games people play is by using the Game Plan. [5] The Game Plan is based on the understanding that each psychological game has a plan of action, much like the kinds of plans that are designed for football plays. It focuses on predictable patterns and payoffs. The basic technique is to ask a series of questions.

- What keeps happening over and over again that leaves someone feeling bad?

- How does the transaction start?

- What happens next?

- And then what happens?

- How does it end?

- How does the initiator feel after it ends—sad, mad, scared, or what?

- How might the other person feel?

EXERCISE 2. RECOGNIZING GAMES

To discover a game played in your work group, refer to the Game Plan questions:

- What keeps happening over and over again that leaves someone feeling bad?

- How does the transaction start?

- What happens next?

- How does it end?

- How might each person feel when it ends?

GAMES CAN BE IDENTIFIED

Games are often named with a word or phrase that characterizes a specific move or theme. For example, the name of the game is likely to be Yes, But if the chairperson at a staff meeting presents a problem, solicits solutions, and then shoots down all of the suggestions.

One woman acted out this game by arguing with all of the doctor's suggestions for treatment. "I can't swallow pills," "I don't have transportation," and "I'm afraid of shots" were only a few of her ploys. This woman was not aware that she was playing a game. People seldom are.

The Game of Yes, But

The first move in this game occurs when one person (playing the Victim) presents a problem in the guise of asking advice from someone else. In the second move the other person (playing the Rescuer) advises, "Why don't you . . . ?" In move three the initiator (switching to Persecutor) says, "Yes, but . . . ," then cites "reasons" why the advice won't work. Eventually the advice giver (now feeling like a Victim) gives up and falls silent, feeling put down, rejected, or put off. At this moment each player reinforces a life position taken in childhood. The first person reinforces the position "People can't tell me anything." The second person reinforces the position "People don't appreciate me." One feels victorious over authority, and the other feels rejected or frustrated.

Yes, But starts when one person from the Child ego state attracts the Nurturing Parent in the other. Although the transactions may appear to be Adult to Adult on the surface ("I've got a problem. Tell me the answer"), the ulterior transaction is Child to Parent ("I've got a problem. Just *try* to tell me the answer. I won't let you.")

Yes, But can be diagrammed as follows:

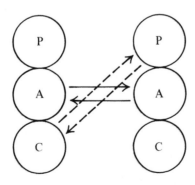

Sender: "I've got a problem. . ."
(Just *try* to tell me the answer. I won't let you.)

Respondent: "Why don't you . . . ?"
(I've got lots of advice.)

A person who plays Yes, But does so to maintain a position such as "Nobody's going to tell me what to do" or "People (authority figures) are stupid." In childhood Yes, But players are likely to have had parents who gave them "all the answers" or who pushed them around or who didn't give any answers and seemed stupid, so they took a stand against their parents—"You're not-OK." Later in life they reinforce this position and are against other authority figures, such as a supervisor, physician, vice-president, or the establishment.

The Game of Kick Me

The game of Kick Me requires a Victim (I'm not-OK) looking for a kick and a Persecutor (You're not-OK) willing to do the kicking. In a mild form of the game the kick could be a dirty look; in a more serious form a beating. It's hard to believe, but it's true that some people get their kicks out of being hurt.

The person who starts the game unknowingly expects to be put down. Usually this person suffers from low self-esteem and uses "cons" to provoke others to reinforce the low self-image.

The game can be diagrammed as follows:

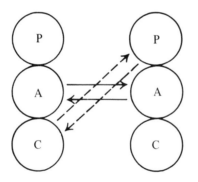

Patient: "Doctor, I keep forgetting to take my pills." (Ulterior: I'm a bad boy, kick me.")

Physician: "Sorry about that. This is the last time I can offer you this treatment on your insurance." (Ulterior: "Yes, you are a bad boy, and here is your kick.")

One fourteen-year-old pregnant girl who felt ugly and unliked complained, "I have to go along with what my boyfriend wants, or I wouldn't have any dates." Her attitude was a "come-on" for her school nurse to lecture her severely about her morals. Thus she found her Persecutor.

Kick Me players often scold themselves with admonitions such as "I could kick myself for saying that." Thus they act as their own persecutors, playing an internal game.

The Game of Stupid

The game of Stupid is similar to Kick Me, and it too is played to collect put-downs. The "kick," however, is related to the person's intelligence and competence. "How could you do such a dumb thing?" is a frequent end to the game.

This game was started by a person who "accidentally" put a medical report in a bottom drawer. Later, when it was discovered, he made a fuss, complaining, "How could I have done such a stupid thing! This was the report that you wanted to send to the insurance company last month."

One woman was a real victim of a Stupid player when she had the wrong leg prepared for surgery. Another lay on the delivery table while aides searched for her file, which lay in the back seat of her physician's car. Anyone might make a mistake; however, when mistakes are repetitive, it's a sign of a game.

A twist to Stupid occurs in the game of Schlemiel, which is usually acted out by the player's being clumsy and making destructive messes. Rather than expecting a kick, however, the person wants forgiveness. "Love me no matter what I do." One person acted out Schlemiel by spilling and breaking things, then apologizing so profusely that the supervisor felt compelled to respond with, "Don't worry. I'll clean it up."

The Game of See What You Made Me Do

See What You Made Me Do players place the blame on others and then feel self-righteous. A receptionist played this game by making a mistake at the typewriter while the office nurse watched from behind. Then, rather than taking responsibility for the error, the receptionist turned to the nurse, angrily saying, "See What You Made Me Do!" thus placing the blame elsewhere. This happened so often that the nurse collected enough hurt feelings to eventually stay away from the front desk. Thus the receptionist, with righteous indignation, got the game's payoff, which was *isolation.*

One surgeon acted out the same blaming game by dropping an instrument in surgery and then giving the assistant an angry, icy glare. A ten-year-old boy played See What You Made Me Do, but collected feelings of purity instead of anger. He was overheard in emergency, accusing his mother, "It's your fault I bashed my finger. You told me to 'hurry up.' "

The Game of Let's You and Him Fight

Another game in which people collect white stamps and feelings of self-righteousness is Let's You and Him Fight. This game requires three players and is initiated by someone who is usually fearful of direct confrontation or who enjoys seeing others make fools of themselves, so sets up two other people to fight.

A common form of this game was observed when a nurse received conflicting orders from two doctors. She privately told each that she couldn't follow directions because the other doctor's directions were different. The two doctors then got into an argument over lines of authority and treatment; the nurse took the day off with a "sick headache." [6]

Let's You and Him Fight is intensified when the organizational chart is ignored, when it says that there is one person to report to when in fact there are several, or when lines of authority are confused or unclear. It may also be played as a serious game, as when contracts are negotiated and administration is pitted against organized (or disorganized) labor.

The Game of Lunch Bag

Lunch Bag is a favorite game of persons in power positions who stress purity and self-righteousness. This game was played by an administrator who consistently brought her lunch—usually last night's leftovers—to work in a little brown bag. Then she sat cloistered in her office while other staff members went out for their hour-long lunch break. When they passed by her door, they often felt a twinge of guilt.

In a variation of Lunch Bag, the members of a small hospital unit frequently had their staff meetings at lunch time, complete with fast-food sandwiches. They thereby sacrificed their break and let others know how much they had to put up with.

A person playing this game uses the self-righteous position to manipulate and control others. The game wards off "frivolous" demands. The ulterior message is: "If important people like us can be this frugal, so can you."

The Game of Harried

People often act out a game of Harried to justify an eventual collapse or depression. People who play Harried say "yes" to every task, volunteer to come early and work late, take on after-hours assignments, and carry work home. This game can structure many years of a person's life, and for a period of time, at least, they are able to act like supermen or superwomen. Eventually, however, their appearance begins to reflect their harried state, and they fold up, unable to meet their obligations. When this happens, they may come to work a bit disheveled, perhaps unkempt or with bloodshot eyes. They may be unable to finish their work. Their physical and mental health deteriorates. They collect so many feelings of depression that they finally cash them in by collapsing.

This game is a natural for people in health care. There is the Harried Patient ("Between work and family, I'm exhausted"), Harried Doctor ("I'm the only one around here who can do it; I'll stay tonight, too"), Harried Clerk ("I'm frantic trying to find the charts everyone needs; I even take a short lunch hour"), and Harried Nurse ("I always run, run from one crisis to another"). A script of an organization often calls for Harried players, and eventually everybody loses. One common result of Harried is burnout—pushing oneself for "the cause" until the limit is reached.

Harried Health Care can be continued in many ways—by limiting a patient's self-responsibility and increasing dependency, by playing "I'm so indispensable" and not delegating tasks to others, by doing innumerable "patch-up jobs," dealing with symptoms but not advising a healthier lifestyle to remove the causes. Harrieds often play the Rescuer role, but end up as Victims.

Harried is a dangerous game.

The Game of Rapo

Some games have sexual overtones. One game most people have seen, at least in the movies, is Rapo. A woman who plays a game of Rapo follows specific moves which lead to a predictable ending. She first baits a man with sexy behavior (Child to Child ulterior), perhaps while they are discussing a recent organizational crisis (plausible Adult to Adult transaction), and then cuts him down when he is attracted to the bait. Her ulterior message is: "I'm available," even though she has no intention of being available. Instead, she wants to prove an early childhood decision: "Men are not-OK. They're sex fiends, only after 'one thing.'"

One day an LVN became aware of the bait she was offering by wearing a very short skirt; as she leaned way over the bed to straighten a sheet, the patient reached up and patted her on the thigh. When she acted indignant, he retorted, "Look, I don't mean any harm. If you put it in front of me, I'm going to grab it. Don't offer what you don't intend to give."

A similar game, called <u>Kiss-off</u>, occurs when a man "butters up" a woman and then drops her cold just when she shows interest (<u>Kiss-off</u>)—perhaps turning his attentions to another woman. This drama reinforces his early childhood belief that women are not-OK. The initial ulterior transaction of both of these games can be diagrammed as follows.

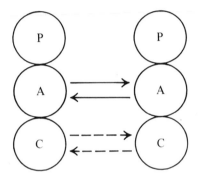

There are many nonsexual games that have the same dynamic as <u>Rapo</u>. An invitation is given or promise is made that serves as the bait. Then if someone goes for the bait, it is withdrawn, with words such as, "I don't know where you got that idea" or "You must have misunderstood. That's not what I meant." When a person in personnel acts this out, it is usually with an unrealistic promise about the job's requirements, benefits, or potential for promotion.

Other Popular Games

Following are the themes of other popular games:

- <u>Cornered</u>: "If I don't prescribe pills, I'm not helping you. If I do, I'm asking you to take a risk. I'm damned if I do and damned if I don't."

- <u>Blemish</u>: "Your last report was very good; *however,* on page 4 you used a comma where you should have used a semicolon."

- "<u>I'm Only Trying to Help You</u>": "So this new drug caused you to become impotent. Don't get so upset. I was only trying to help you."

- <u>Ain't It Awful</u>: "Oh, this is terrible. There's a new cure for the disease! What'll we do now? We have all these fund-raising pamphlets!"

- Wooden Leg: "Surely you can't expect much from me when I have such a handicap." (I'm the wrong sex, wrong size, wrong race, wrong background, have low-back pain, come from a broken home, etc.)

- See How Hard I Tried: "Don't blame me if this procedure isn't successful. After all, see how hard I tried."

- Uproar: "You stupid fool, you never do anything right."

- Now I've Got You, You S.O.B.: You've made a big mistake this time, and now you're going to suffer for it!"

- Psychiatry: "If you'd stop playing games with me and come on less Parent, I'd get along just fine!"

EXERCISE 3. DISCOVERING GAMES

Select four games mentioned above that "ring a bell" with you. Discuss how each is acted out in your particular work group. If you are in a large organization, talk about how one or two of these games might be played on a larger scale. For each game, discuss:

- What role the person who starts the game is likely playing—Victim, Persecutor, or Rescuer.

- What kinds of feelings and stamps are collected by the parties involved in the games.

- Whether some of these games seem to fit together (e.g., Kick Me and Blemish). If so, which ones?

- What games health personnel might be likely to play.

- What games health care recipients might be likely to play.

Now select two common games and role-play them.

PEOPLE CAN GIVE UP GAMES

People who decide to give up their games first need to become aware of how games are initiated. People need to recognize them, to identify roles in them, to interrupt them, to avoid them, and eventually to give them up. In giving up their games they learn to give and to accept *positive strokes*. They learn to structure their time more appropriately to meet current goals. They get in touch with their potentials to relate well to others rather than devoting their energies to "acting" the hurting parts that games require. They learn to focus on really *solving problems* rather than going in circles with old dialogue.

There are many ways to stop a game once people know that they are playing. For example, refusing to give advice or suggestions to a Yes, But player usually stops that game. Refusing to feel bad when criticized interrupts a Kick Me game. Refusing to be defensive stops the Uproar game. Other techniques a person can use are:

- Give an unexpected response.

- Stop exaggerating his or her own weaknesses or strengths.

- Stop exaggerating the weaknesses and strengths of others.

- Give and receive positive strokes rather than negative strokes.

- Stop playing Rescuer—helping those who don't need or want help.

- Stop playing Persecutor—criticizing those who don't need or want it.

- Stop playing Victim—acting helpless or dependent when really able to stand on one's own two feet.

- Turn energy to defining and solving problems.

EXERCISE 4. GAME AWARENESS

Now go back to a game recognized in Exercise 3. Discuss what each person could do differently *at each step* (especially step two) that could stop the game:

How can health care be improved by being aware of games?

What are the consequences of playing fewer games?

- In client care?

- In staff effectiveness?

EXERCISE 5. BREAKING UP GAMES

Assume that of all the players, only one person had "game consciousness" and wanted to break the game. What steps could that person take?

What effect might it have on other players?

Now act out the game of Yes, But. Select people for the parts and role-play various ways to break up this game. If time allows, role-play other games common to health care settings.

SUMMARY

Games most often are negative scenes in people's life dramas. People play games in an unaware way to reinforce old childhood decisions and to act out their psychological scripts. Players get strokes (though they may be negative), structure their time (though it may be wasteful), reinforce their psychological positions (though they may be irrational), and further their scripts (though they may be self-defeating). People also feel justified in cashing in old resentments (though these are acts of over-self-indulgence) and thus avoid authentic encounters (even though they may be acting as if that's what they want). But perhaps most important, since games deal with old programming, they prevent solving *current* problems. When problems go unrecognized, ignored, and unsolved, everyone suffers.

Destructive games can be recognized and given up. Then time and energy are freed up for problem solving. Positive strokes are given and received and the possibility for authenticity and genuine caring allowed to emerge. A healthier, more open environment leads to a clarity of communication that in turn promotes even more winning ways in health care.

UNIT 6

EGO STATE BLOCKS TO PROBLEM SOLVING

Have you dealt with people:

- who seem to be rigid and continually act dependent, authoritarian, or coldly objective?

- who seem to be highly prejudiced, have "made up their minds and don't want to be confused by the facts"?

- who seem unable to separate fact from fantasy?

- whose emotions keep them from solving their problems?

If you have, you have observed some of the effects that ego state boundary problems can have on personality. Boundary problems interfere with many capacities, such as thinking clearly, finding new options for old problems, recognizing and dealing with feelings appropriately, and responding to others in satisfying ways. Understanding ego state boundary problems increases understanding of why people do what they do.

EGO STATES HAVE BOUNDARIES

People with boundary problems are usually not aware of the effects their personalities have on others. They may not be able to identify changes that need to be made. When they do, they feel powerless to change them. This inability to change negative situations contributes to chronic poor health or accident-proneness, fatigue and burnout, "flying off the handle," passive-aggressive behavior or withdrawal, or sometimes even death.

Berne says that ego state boundaries are like semipermeable membranes through which psychic energy can flow from one ego state to another. Ego boundaries need to be semipermeable because otherwise, psychic energy becomes locked into one ego state, unable to move to another ego state in response to changing situations.

There are four ego state boundary problems: lax, lesions, contamination, and exclusion. These can be severe pathological problems [1] or can be experienced at a much less intense level.

SOME PEOPLE HAVE LAX PERSONALITIES

When people have lax ego state boundaries, they cannot stay in the ego state that is appropriate to a specific situation. They lack self-control, since the boundaries between their ego states are partially open. This problem is most easily observable on the back wards of state mental hospitals—in patients who show little or no Adult functioning, appear to lack identity, and give the impression of being somewhat sloppy in appearance, thinking, and behavior.

In general, people with extreme lax ego boundary problems tend to be careless, unreliable, and unpredictable. Because of their own lack of control, they have difficulty being effective in relating to others. One patient who experienced this problem was described by the orderly as "so hard to understand; you never know what's going on with him or what he's going to do next."

At a less severe level, a patient or staff member with this problem may function (though unpredictably), relating to others in minimally satisfying ways, but making poor choices when he or she needs to make decisions. A personality with lax boundaries is sometimes defined as slipshod and can be diagrammed as follows:

People with this problem sometimes change if they receive a high number of strokes for Adult thinking and appropriate behavior. One social service worker with a daughter who had lax ego boundaries discovered that giving her daughter Adult information, without critical or nurturing transactions, was the most effective way to strengthen her ego state boundaries.

EXERCISE 1. THE LAX PERSONALITY TYPE

Think of a person you have known who seemed to have lax ego state boundaries.

• What is your relationship like with that person?

• How do you often feel around that person?

• How might that person feel around you?

• What kinds of transactions seem to be ineffective with that person?

• What kinds of transactions seem to be the most effective with that person?

SORE SPOTS ARE LESIONS

Persons who have ego boundary lesions exhibit uncontrollable behavior when their "sore spots" are touched. This problem is often manifested by a gross over-reaction to the reality of the stimulus. A person faints at the sight of a mouse, gets hysterical over a clap of thunder, panics and hides at the thought of performing, and so forth. Some people break into tears or sink into depressions when even mildly criticized. [2]

Usually people with lesions have been seriously injured by traumatic events or by a series of unhappy experiences during childhood. When something rubs the sore spot, the injury may "break open," with the person outpouring strong, irrational emotion. This was observed in a staff meeting when one person told another, "I would like it if you would look at me when you speak to me!" At this simple request the second person exploded in rage, ending the outburst by yelling, "You really know how to make me mad!"

Occasionally lesions are sore spots in the Parent, but they are most likely to be sore spots in the Child. Boundary lesions can be diagrammed like this:

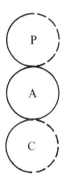

One of the reasons why some physicians and nurses avoid talking to a terminally ill patient about death is their fear of opening a lesion in the patient or perhaps in themselves. This seems to be the case in the following poignant news report:

The man's wife died soon after she suffered a stroke and was taken to the hospital in an ambulance. "Sure, I know the doctors and nurses were busy trying to save her," he says.

But when it was over they just wheeled her out and someone told me that she was dead. No one said that they were sorry, or asked if they could do anything for me. They just looked away when I started to cry." He pauses. "They left me standing there all alone." [3]

Being alone or avoided in a crisis is not unusual. As one nurse shared, "Lesions are the reasons no one can be found to tell a family that the patient died, or the newborn baby has a birth defect, or that the disease is terminal."

Few people want to be the bearers of bad news. Such tasks are often left to a hospital chaplain, a pastoral counselor, or a family member. Studies show that a large percentage of troubled or fearful people often seek out pastoral counselors before seeking psychological or physical health care. These counselors may be the only persons willing to counsel them through a crisis of illness or impending death. [4] However, more and more focus is being placed on dealing openly with dying patients. This is an attempt to heal a sore spot that is fairly common to the script of the larger culture.

EXERCISE 2. THE FEAR OF SORE SPOTS

Discuss two typical situations in health care in which people may fear hitting a sore spot.

● Are these fears well founded or not?

● If not, what could be done to lessen the fear?

- How could a chaplain or a counselor assist the staff to become more effective?

EXERCISE 3. RIGHTS OF A DYING PERSON

Read through the following, "The Dying Person's Bill of Rights," as developed by the Southwestern Michigan Inservice Education Council. [5]

THE DYING PERSON'S BILL OF RIGHTS

I have the right to be treated as a living human being until I die.

I have the right to maintain a sense of hopefulness, however changing its focus may be.

I have the right to be cared for by those who can maintain a sense of hopefulness, however changing this might be.

I have the right to express my feelings and emotions about my approaching death, in my own way.

I have the right to participate in decisions concerning my case.

I have the right to expect continuing medical and nursing attention even though "cure" goals must be changed to "comfort" goals.

I have the right not to die alone.

I have the right to be free from pain.

I have the right to have my questions answered honestly.

I have the right not to be deceived.

I have the right to have help from and for my family in accepting my death.

I have the right to die in peace and dignity.

I have the right to retain my individuality and not be judged for my decisions, which may be contrary to the beliefs of others.

I have the right to discuss and enlarge my religious and/or spiritual experiences, regardless of what they may mean to others.

I have the right to expect that the sanctity of the human body will be respected after death.

I have the right to be cared for by caring, sensitive, knowledgeable people who will attempt to understand my needs and will be able to gain some satisfaction in helping me face my death.

Discuss each item above. Are they recognized as rights in your work setting? If not, does it point to some "sore spots" that need healing?

SOME PEOPLE SHOW EGO STATE PREFERENCE

Rigid ego state boundaries are observable in people who are "overly" predictable, seldom showing any spontaneity. They may continually act like critical or nurturing parents or like rebellious, obedient, or inadequate children or like robot-type, computing grownups. They may have excluded one or two of their ego states.

When people overuse their Parent ego state or their Child ego state and do not use their Adult, they are not in touch with the current situation. They are replaying what happened in the past or rehearsing for what might happen in the future. Living in the past or future increases body tension. In contrast, if people exclude their Parent and Child ego states, using only their Adult, they may be bores or robots without passion or compassion.

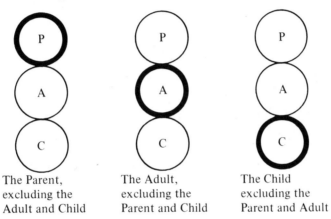

The Parent, excluding the Adult and Child

The Adult, excluding the Parent and Child

The Child excluding the Parent and Adult

Rigidly responding from only one ego state may cause serious communication problems which could be decreased with professional help. However, many people *favor* one ego state over the other. This is less serious, but still presents a problem—the problem of being constantly Parent, constantly Adult, or constantly Child. The helping professions sometimes attract the person who favors the use of the Parent.

Some People Prefer Their Parent Ego State

People who overuse the Parent may lack certain competencies or creative spontaneity. They often treat others, even business associates, as if they were children. Such behavior can be found in secretaries who "take care of" everyone's problems in the office or in organization executives who try to run everyone's personal lives, or in physicians or nurses who are always "on duty" in their professional roles. They cannot be approached reasonably and display little or no sense of humor. Either knowingly or unknowingly, the constant Parent collects people who are willing to be dependent, submissive, or subordinate.

In the health care setting, effective patient care is hindered when self-responsibility is not encouraged. For example, patients might unnecessarily give up their decision-making and problem-solving processes to others, especially if they are encouraged to do so unnecessarily. A typical response of one physician, when questioned by patients about X-rays, was a condescending "Now we don't want to get upset over something like an X-ray, do we?"

One type of Constant Parent is hard working, has a strong sense of duty, and often seeks a position of power. Sometimes these persons become Persecutors—judgmental, critical, and moralistic. They want others to obey without question.

Another type of Constant Parent is the perpetual nurturer or Rescuer, who may act like a benevolent dictator. Sometimes such people overindulge their own nurturing capacities and neglect keeping current in their field. They focus on "caring" *at the expense of* "curing." In the words of one physician describing such a colleague: "He has a great bedside manner, but has trouble passing the boards."

EXERCISE 4. THE CONSTANT PARENT IN ACTION

People who favor their Parent ego state tend to hold firmly to their traditions and prejudices. They are attracted to certain jobs, people, and situations. Discuss the following:

Vocations preferred by
Constant Parent

Kinds of people
they attract

Games they
might play

Kinds of strokes
they tend to give

Kinds of strokes
they tend to get

Script themes
they might act out

Some People Prefer Their Adult Ego State

Some people who function primarily as Constant Adults are consistently objective, uninvolved, and concerned primarily with facts and data processing. They may appear unfeeling, lack sympathy, and seem uninterested in another person's pain. Not only are their nurturing qualities lacking, but also they show little capacity for fun, spontaneity, and are likely to be bores at parties. One doctor described such a colleague as "a medical genius who is a beast with people."

People who exhibit the rigid boundary problem of the Constant Adult sometimes seem cold if they've chosen a people-oriented job. They seem to relate better to objects and may overuse gadgets and technology. For example, the emotions of some surgeons, operating room nurses, and other acute-care personnel may be so blocked that a patient may feel that the experience was void of human contact. One patient in such a situation recalled, "It was like a weird dream. There were lights and all kinds of machinery and gadgets. I could hear people talking to each other, but no one spoke to me or even acknowledged that I was there. I've never felt so alone and so disconnected." Another patient recalled, "When I was in the critical-care unit, someone came in every five or ten minutes to check the machines, but seldom checked me. I wish they would have at least patted me on the shoulder."

The Constant Adult often experiences trouble on a job if supervising others is a requirement of the position. With little caring Parent or fun-loving Child, relationships are likely to be sterile. Subordinates may be unhappy because they receive so little stroking. Many work situations suffer if there is no one acting as a nurturing, caring Parent and no one to "joke around with," like a child.

EXERCISE 5. THE CONSTANT ADULT IN ACTION

People who favor their Adult ego state tend to hold firmly to "hard facts and rational thinking." They tend to be attracted to certain styles, people, and behavior. Discuss the following:

Vocations preferred by Constant Adult	*Kinds of people they attract*	*Games they might play*
Kinds of strokes they tend to give	*Kinds of strokes they tend to get*	*Script themes they might act out*

Some People Prefer Their Child Ego State

The person who functions primarily as Constant Child is the one who is the perpetual little boy or girl and who, like Peter Pan, doesn't want to grow up. Such people may fail to think for themselves, to make their own decisions, and to take personal responsibility. They may, if not withdrawn, go for the spotlight—in either negative or positive ways. Often they are highly self-centered, do not think clearly, and are poor at providing direct care to others.

   People using a Constant Child show little or no conscience in their dealings with other people and usually attach themselves to others who will "take care of" them. A man or woman who wants to be "kept," babied, punished or rewarded, or continually applauded is likely to seek out a Constant Parent who agrees to the arrangement. Patients who show this problem may seek an overly sympathetic nurse or doctor. They assume little or no responsibility for self-care and shift heavy responsibility to other people.

EXERCISE 6. THE CONSTANT CHILD IN ACTION

People who favor their Child ego state often procrastinate or are overly compliant or rebellious. Their dependency patterns may keep them in subordinate positions or in low-paying jobs that have no future. Discuss the following:

Vocations preferred by
Constant Child

Kinds of people they
attract

Games they might
play

Kinds of strokes they
tend to give

Kinds of strokes they
tend to get

Script themes they
might act out

EXERCISE 7. YOUR EGO STATE PORTRAIT

Using circles of different sizes, imagine your ego state portrait as you perceive yourself functioning most of the time. Your portrait might look something like one of the figures below:

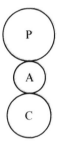 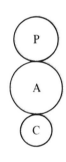 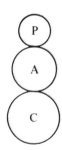

Draw yours here:

• Do you see yourself as having a favorite ego state?

- Does your portrait change when the situation changes? At work? At home? At school? At a party? Where else?

- Does it change with certain people? A boss? A patient? A peer? A child? An elderly person? Who else?

- Now ask a child, spouse, friend, relative, or co-worker to draw how he or she perceives you. Notice any differences?

After you have drawn your ego state portraits, both from your own perspective and that of others, ask yourself:

- Does this satisfy me? If not, what needs to be changed?

- What decisions do I need to make? What data do I need to gather?

ADULT THINKING CAN BE CONTAMINATED

The clear thinking of the Adult is often spoiled by *contamination*. When this occurs, rational problem solving is blocked. Contamination can be thought of as an intrusion of the Parent and/or the Child into the boundary of the Adult. Contamination occurs when the Adult accepts as *true* some unfounded Parent beliefs or Child distortions and rationalizes and justifies these attitudes.

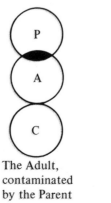

The Adult, contaminated by the Parent

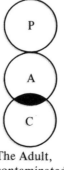

The Adult, contaminated by the Child

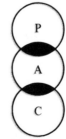

The Adult, contaminated by the Parent and Child

In extreme cases, contamination from the Parent is experienced as hallucinations, which are *sensory* perception of things that are not real. [6] Persons are hallucinating when they see something that is not there or when they imagine that they hear voices that accuse or command. As one man claimed, "I castrated myself because my inner voice told me to."

To a lesser degree, Parent contaminations are prejudices—tenaciously held opinions which have not been examined on the basis of objective data. Parental figures often express their prejudices to children with such conviction that they appear to be facts. The person who believes these Parental opinions without evaluating them has a contaminated Adult.

Severe contamination from the Child ego state often occurs because of some delusion. Common ones are the delusions of grandeur (exaggerating one's importance) or persecution ("Everyone's out to get me"). When people *feel* as if no one likes them, yet have no objective data that this is so, they are experiencing a common contamination. They believe that their feelings represent the truth about themselves and do not believe compliments or genuine gestures of friendship.

Other common ways the Child contaminates the Adult is with the distortions that come from the script. People's beliefs about themselves, their self-concepts, and personal expectations are often not accurate in terms of their real possibilities. These script decisions, which are in the Adapted Child, distort a person's clear thinking and are likely to be reinforced by the Parent. "I *never* do anything right" would be a Child contamination because everyone does some things right, and use of the word "never" is an exaggeration. An inner voice syaing, "You *never* do anything right" is the Parent reinforcement.

Like the word "never", the word "*always*" ("you *always* drag your feet when it's time to clean up") is a similar clue to contamination.

EXERCISE 8. STEREOTYPES AS CONTAMINATIONS

Contaminations show most obviously in the prejudices people have and the stereotypes they use. List at least five descriptive adjectives and/or phrases that are common stereotypes.

Women are: *Men are:*

Discuss how these attitudes might affect job choice and expected performance.
Now identify commonly held beliefs about various health care personnel.

Physicians are: *Nurses are:*

Technicians are: *Administrators are:*

Discuss how beliefs like those above may affect life goals, choice of associates, unrealistic expectations of self and others, patterns of communication on the job, and possible discrimination.

EXERCISE 9. ADJECTIVES TELL A STORY

Write the names of three people you dislike or avoid. Then, without censoring your thoughts, list five descriptive words that come to mind when you think of each person.

_____   _____   _____

Now compare these lists. Is there any similarity of adjectives?

Do the people you've selected seem similar to one another?

Do your words reflect a prejudice against people of a certain age? Race? Sex? Position?

Would your attitudes have any effect on patient care?

THE ADULT CAN BE STRENGTHENED

Contaminated thinking can be cleared up when people are given facts in ways that are understandable to them. Facts strengthen the Adult ego state. When the Adult is strong, contamination is reduced, open and lax boundaries may be closed, emotional lesions may heal, and rigid ego state boundaries may loosen up to allow a freer flow of energy. The Adult is strengthened with use.

One of the Adult's major uses is problem solving. Sometimes people would like to change jobs, change behavior patterns, improve family relationships, be tolerant of more people, consider more education, etc., but feel that they don't dare. By exercising the use of the Adult, they become more willing to take risks and to develop new strategies for change.

EXERCISE 10. DECONTAMINATING FOR PROBLEM SOLVING

Problems can be solved much more efficiently when the attitudes, beliefs, and feelings of each ego state are sorted out. Fill in the following personal inventory.

A problem I need to solve is:

My Parent ego state involvement:

- What might each of my parent figures *say* about this kind of problem?

- What might each of them *do* about it?

My Child ego state involvement:

- How does my Child feel about the problem?

- What games might I play in connection with the problem?

- Does my involvement fit my script in some way?

My Adult ego state evaluation:

- What in my Parent helps me?

- What in my Parent hinders me?

- What in my Child helps me?

- What in my Child hinders me?

- Do I need more facts before making a decision?

- If so, how can I get the facts?

Be aware of possible effects of your decision. A decision that makes you feel uncomfortable may have your Parent and/or Child fighting against it, may actually be harmful to you or others, or may be simply the wrong decision.

EXERCISE 11. PERSONALITY FACTORS IN PROBLEM SOLVING

Define a problem and then list the major factors that center on the problem you want to solve or the decision you want to make. For example, if you are considering a move, factors might include such things as recreational possibilities, pay, or distance from your relatives.

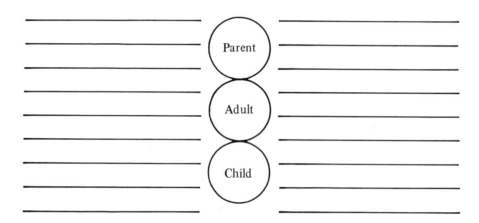

Now go back over each factor and decide which ego state that particular factor is most related to. Draw a line from each factor to each ego state. If one factor fits about the same for two or more ego states, draw lines to all. After you have completed this task, consider the following questions.

• Are only one or two ego states predominant in your consideration of this problem? Is this appropriate?

• Are you going against any particular ego state? If so, which one?

- How much is your Adult involved in solving this problem? In what ways? Is this an appropriate amount?

- How much is your Child involved in this problem? In what ways? Is this an appropriate amount?

- How much is your Parent involved in this problem? In what ways? Is this an appropriate amount?

Now, as a group, discuss a problem that exists in your organization. Go through the same questions as they relate to the organizational ego states.

SUMMARY

A person's spontaneous use of personality resources can be affected by ego boundary problems. Ego boundaries can be too lax or too rigid. If too lax, the personality seems out of control or is affected by lesions which result in irrational outbursts. If too rigid, the psychic energy is "locked" into one ego state, excluding the others. This problem manifests itself by a continuous use of one ego state—the person chooses to act almost exclusively from the Parent, the Adult, or the Child. The Adult's clear perception of current reality can also be contaminated by prejudiced beliefs and childhood delusions.

For the Adult to gain executive control so that the person can solve problems, this ego state must be activated and used. Everyone has this potential. Berne makes the analogy that a person may have a good radio, but it needs to be turned on and tuned in before it can be heard clearly. [7] When your Adult ego state is turned on and tuned in, it can help you set the course of your job and your life in even more winning ways.

UNIT 7

STRUCTURING TIME AND CONTRACTING FOR CHANGE

Have you observed people who:

- act distant and detached even when they are with others?

- speak and act in stereotyped ways that may have generations of tradition behind them?

- pass time talking about inconsequential matters?

- gleefully "catch" others when they make a mistake?

- work together as a team to get a task completed?

- experience intimacy and closeness with one another?

If so, you have observed the six ways people structure their time when they are with others: withdrawal, rituals, pastimes, games, activities, and intimacy.*

PEOPLE HUNGER FOR STRUCTURE

Just as people experience a hunger for strokes, they also experience a hunger to structure their time. This hunger may be satisfied in several ways. The amount of time and energy devoted to each way often reflects a script—how the drama of a lifetime is structured. For example, people in destructive scripts use much of their time playing games. Those in going-nowhere scripts devote a great deal of their time to rituals and pastimes. Those with constructive, winning scripts invest time in activities and intimacy.

Withdrawal

Withdrawal can be physical or psychological, positive or negative. Among members of a staff group, people may withdraw *physically* from others because they want to avoid a confrontation, a discussion, a request, an extra task, or because they want to be somewhere else, doing something else.

Some people withdraw *emotionally* by letting their minds go blank or engaging in fantasies such as: "If I were Chief of Staff, I'd run this meeting differently" or "If I had a million dollars, I'd never work again." They may daydream about something they hope to do some day: "Maybe I'll catch the limit fishing this weekend" or someplace they want to be: "If only I were on a different ward" or about some future plan of action: "One of these days, I'll tell that S.O.B. a thing or two."

Psychological withdrawal is common not only when people are bored, but also when people are afraid. For example, during a self-examination, Irma found a lump in her breast. Normally, she was the life of the party, a leader of neighborhood events, and a well-liked secretary. For two weeks, Irma suspected possible cancer, but told herself, "It could never happen to me." She needed to have it checked out, but felt afraid to share that kind of a problem with anyone, so she chose to withdraw, to be quiet and not talk. Irma avoided friends, outwardly maintained a "stiff upper lip," yet inwardly was frightened and confused. Finally, after many fearful days, she went to her physician, who urged immediate biopsy.

Withdrawn patients like Irma are frequently found in hospitals, clinics, and geriatric settings. So are staff who may respond likewise, using the rationale that it's better to "leave well enough alone."

---

* Berne discusses the six ways of structuring time in *relationships*. We are broadening this idea to include how people structure their *life's time.*

Many times psychological withdrawal leads to communication problems. For example, someone may not hear important instructions or important feedback or the "real" request that lies behind a person's superficial remarks or silence.

At other times psychological withdrawal is essential to health. For example, a patient may need to withdraw in order for the healing process to begin. Efforts to "cheer up" the person may discount his or her deeper feelings and needs. In a similar way, a nurse or doctor may need to withdraw to find a quiet corner and just relax or to explore his or her own feelings and needs. Moments of quiet withdrawal can renew body, mind, or spirit.

Rituals

Ritual transactions are simple, stereotyped, complementary transactions like everyday "hellos" and "goodbyes." If people in social situations say, "Good morning, how are you?" they are seldom inquiring into the other person's health and feelings. Instead, they expect a ritualistic response, "Fine, how are you?" In this brief encounter both persons get strokes. The strokes may not be intense, but they serve the purpose of giving and getting recognition. In health care situations this question may not be a ritual but have a more straightforward meaning.

Rituals are often tied to family, organizational, and cultural scripts. For example, one hospital patient wanted warm milk to help him sleep, just as he'd had every evening in his family. One nurse expected to "automatically" dispense sleeping pills to all patients, as she had been instructed to do in another hospital. Another patient demanded wine with his lunch, claiming, "I can always get it in my country."

The use of rituals can be highly effective because people can count on what's going to happen. Some rituals add order, predictability, and comfort to people's lives. For example, religious rituals are very important to patients who find in them spiritual support, solace, and sometimes healing.

Some routines become rituals that serve a helpful purpose—as, for example, a nurse making rounds with a physician in a hospital. Other routine rituals, however, may be counterproductive, such as a meeting for only RNs or LVNs or nurses' assistants, without ever getting the "healing" team together. Rituals need to be constantly reexamined so that time is not spent going through thoughtless, meaningless motions.

Pastimes

Pastiming, another common way of spending time, often follows a ritualistic greeting. When pastiming, people simply talk to one another about subjects that are of little consequence. One of the most common conversational pastimes is the weather. "Gee, it sure is hot." "Yeah, summer's coming," or "Boy, that wind has a chill in it," or "Maybe it's going to snow tonight." Any subject can be used as a pastime—friends, scars, drugs, length of labor, emergency experiences, personal gossip, cars, vacation trips, and so forth.

One common pastime is "Ain't It Awful." Many lunch breaks are structured with some talk about how awful someone or something is, without any intention of doing anything about it. "Ain't it awful about the budget cut, the lack of personnel, the long hours we put in, or the scandal involving John and Marcia."

The reverse of this is "Ain't It Wonderful." After a successful and delicate transplant, people may pass some time lauding the operating room staff with, "Weren't they wonderful!" (And they probably were!)

Sometimes pastimes waste time. For example, nothing productive may come out of an exchange about the weather or who drives the best car. However, during pastimes people's Little Professor intuitively "psyche out" one another for possible fun, companionship, and even game playing. Also, people get acquainted and can perhaps learn about common interests which might lead to a deeper relationship. Yet people who stay at a pastime level never get to know others really well. They are good at "small talk" but have little depth in their transactions.

Games

Games are the least productive ways people use time. Games always result in someone's feeling bad because people unknowingly play them to get and give negative strokes. Games tend to be unproductive because they are ulterior and are played to avoid solving problems, making decisions, and getting close to people.

Structuring time with games often indicates that the players are involved in reliving their negative feelings of the past and are reinforcing their old not-OK positions rather than being involved in what's going on right now. Sometimes games start when expected rituals or pastimes are ignored. For example, in some hospitals an expected ritual is for a nurse to stand when a physician comes onto the ward. A game of Blemish or Now I've Got You, You S.O.B. may start if a nurse drops this ritual.

Games also start when staff members who believe that they "have no time" for the social graces refuse to spend a few minutes pastiming. "Can't you see I'm busy! I can't take time for the office party." When positive strokes are in short supply, games can always stir things up. Even the negative strokes offered by games seem better than none. People will do almost anything for excitement.

Activities

Activities are ways of structuring time that deal with external reality and are commonly thought of as *work*, getting something done. Activities are often what people want to do, need to do, or have to do, such as interviewing a potential staff member, prepping a patient, performing an operation, programming a computer, dispensing medication, developing the X-rays, writing a report, drawing blood, fixing a tray, dictating a letter, and cleaning the floor.

In the midst of the activity of getting a job done, rituals, pastimes, games, and even intimacy may occur. For example, while running a well-baby clinic (activity), two nurses greet each other (ritual), talk about the humid weather (pastime), glance at each other teary-eyed and smile at the sight of a child regaining consciousness (intimacy), go silent at coffee break while thinking of their own children (withdrawal), then later in the day point out an inconsequential mistake (Blemish).

Intimacy

At a deeper level of human encounter than rituals, pastimes, games, and activities lies the potential that each person has for *intimacy*. Time invested in experiencing intimacy is free of games and free of exploitation. It occurs in those rare moments of human contact that arouse feelings of tenderness, empathy, and affection. Intimacy involves genuine caring for the other person and a willingness to be open, even vulnerable.

Any activities, such as going to a meeting, planning patient treatment, conferring with a family, or working on a proposal, serve as contexts for intimacy to occur. The sense of intimacy can happen between strangers or in a continuing relationship. However, people can live or work together for many years, yet never really "see" or "hear" or know each other.

In modern life intimacy seems rare. People who feel crowded in one way or another often seek "psychological" space. They may withdraw or resort to ritualistic living and use "keeping your distance" techniques. Even when jammed into a crowded elevator, they remain distant, pretending not to see one another.

One pediatric nurse lets her small patients know that they are seen. She comes into the waiting room herself, greets them personally, and often holds their hands while taking them into the examining room. She also encourages them to bring in a snapshot of themselves and drawings for the office wall. In exchange, she shows them pictures of her family. All of these acts invite closeness and moments of intimacy.

EXERCISE 1. TIME STRUCTURING ON THE JOB

Discuss the six ways in which time is structured on the job. Comment on the actual kinds of behavior used, what kinds of strokes are involved, and what kind of script each fits into:

Method used	Behavior used	Strokes obtained	Destructive? Constructive? Going nowhere?
Withdrawal			
Rituals			
Pastimes			
Games			
Activities			
Intimacy			

Now discuss each way of structuring time and the kind of transaction—complementary, crossed, or ulterior—that are most common to each.

What are three important ways at work that time structuring could be improved?

In what ways could you personally contribute to this improvement?

EXERCISE 2. YOUR USE OF TIME

How do you spend your time? Think of your average workday as a pie. Let each piece of this pie stand for the portion of the day that you spend in a particular way. [1]

- Do you spend your time as in the diagram on the left? Or as in the one on the right?

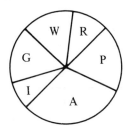
R = Ritual
P = Pastime
A = Activity
G = Game
I = Intimacy
W = Withdrawal
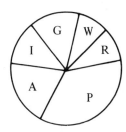

- Divide the pie below into six pieces. Label each piece to show the amount of time you spend in each category.

- Study your diagram. If you're not satisfied with it, use the blank pie on the right to diagram how you would like to spend your time.

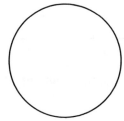
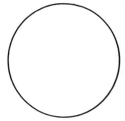

Now consider the kinds of strokes you receive with each way you structure time.

- Are you satisfied with these?

- What, if anything, would you like to be different?

EXERCISE 3. YOUR EGO STATES AND TIME

The purpose of this exercise is to discover how each of your ego states may get involved in the use of time. For your Parent ego state, recall what your parent figures said and did about time. Next, record what you say and do about time when in your Adult. Then get in touch with how you felt about time when you were a child and what you did with it.

My Ego State Involvement

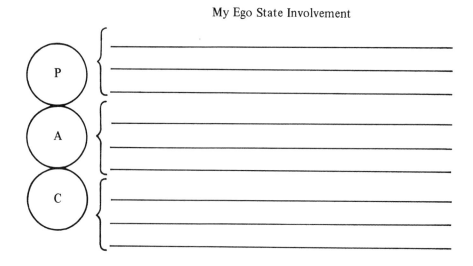

Now evaluate the impact of your ego state programming on the way you use time on your job today.

- Does it fit into your script in some way?

- If you were to receive an inscribed gold watch at your retirement, what would it say, and how would that relate to the way you structure your time at work? [2]

TAKE CHARGE OF YOUR TIME

People structure their time not only in relationships, but also in their lives—from birth to death. Some people pace themselves at high speed like a fine race horse and seem to thrive on it. They may achieve excellence in their work, relax with an absorbing hobby, and maintain satisfying relationships. All too often, however, people in the helping professions invest so much of their time and energy on others that they have little left over for themselves. It seems easy to get caught up in a treadmill of compulsive behavior—always hurrying, trying too hard, doing unimportant things too perfectly, being stoic and strong, continually trying to please, sacrificing themselves for others. [3] One nurse shared, "I haven't sat down for breakfast for years. It seems I'm always eating on the run."

When people act from a compulsion "to hurry up and help," they often do not manage their time so that their own needs get met. Their energy moves outward. Taking little time for revitalization, such people begin to feel burned out.

Burnout results when stress, which is a natural part of activities, becomes *distress.* In fact, Hans Selye describes distress as "harmful, unpleasant stress." [4]

When people experience the impact of distress, they often begin to receive warning signals from their bodies. Such warnings may take the form of irritability, listlessness, resentfulness, anxiety, loneliness, fatigue, or insomnia. Some people never heed these warnings until serious illness strikes and, in effect, forces them to take time for themselves. [5]

People tend to perform most tasks better when they are relaxed. Being relaxed involves taking time to let go. Often this is facilitated by such practices as meditation[6], exercise, and deep-relaxation techniques. [7]

People also perform better when they take time to enjoy themselves and others and recover the ability to laugh. Laughter is physiologically relaxing and healing and is psychologically good therapy. Laughter is indeed good medicine. [8] Because it reduces tension, laughter invites others into moments of intimacy.

People who drive themselves unmercifully often become critical of small talk, jokes, and laughter. They avoid the comic element of life to focus on the tragic.

Health care work is often stressful. When the stress becomes chronic it alienates people from one another and contributes, for example, to coronary disease, hypertension, and mental illness.

People in health care who are concerned about the continuing development of winning ways take time for themselves and avoid the trap of <u>Harried.</u>

EXERCISE 4. STRESS QUIZ

Which Personality Type Are You? [9]

This questionnaire* is designed to help you determine if the personality you bring to work is the reason for most of your stress.

First, go through all thirty statements and rate yourself as to how you typically feel or react in each of the situations.

1 = Never   2 = Seldom   3 = Sometimes   4 = Frequently   5 = Always

1. _____ Meeting new acquaintances is very stressful for me.

2. _____ My spouse or friends think I am hard driving and work too hard.

3. _____ What happens in my life is determined by fate and circumstance.

4. _____ If given the chance, I prefer to work alone.

5. _____ When a job is not clearly laid out for me, I begin to feel anxious.

6. _____ A negative evaluation about my work makes me depressed for days.

7. _____ I pride myself on accomplishing the most work in my department and being the first to meet quotas.

8. _____ Having to make business decisions is particularly stressful for me.

9. _____ There is little I can do to influence the decisions of those in authority.

10. _____ My work is less productive when I have to interact with others.

11. _____ I rely more on other people's opinions than on my own.

12. _____ I would rather have a steady income I can count on than a stimulating but responsible job.

13. _____ I usually work with frequent deadlines and time pressures.

14. _____ Since it is impossible to try to change a large organization, I tend to go along with things as they are.

15. _____ I tend to withdraw from people rather than confront them with problems.

16. _____ If one method for getting the job done works, I am not likely to change it.

17. _____ I need the praise of others to feel I am doing a good job.

---

*   "Which Personality Type are You?" from *Corporate Stress* by Rosalind Forbes, Ed.D. Copyright ©1979 by Rosalind Forbes. Reprinted by permission of Doubleday & Company, Inc.

18. _____ Since I do not want to fail, I avoid risks.

19. _____ I seldom feel good about myself.

20. _____ I become particularly upset with any changes in my routine.

21. _____ I personally do not reveal things about myself.

22. _____ I tend to become overly cautious and anxious in new situations.

23. _____ I have a tendency to produce more and more work in less time.

24. _____ Because of my work, I have no opportunity to do the things I really want to do in life.

25. _____ If someone criticizes me, I begin to doubt myself.

26. _____ I pride myself on being orderly, neat, and punctual.

27. _____ I do not like to go to parties or places where there are a large number of people.

28. _____ Luck has a great deal to do with success.

29. _____ I do a great deal of business during a game of golf or in the course of evening dinners with clients.

30. _____ I become particularly upset if I am contradicted.

For an evaluation of this questionnaire, see Appendix C, p. 149.

EXERCISE 5. YOUR BODY AND YOUR TIME

How does your body generally work? Do you have certain times of day or night when it feels better than others?

* If so, when?

* What is generally going on then?

How do you specifically experience "feeling better"?

Is your body sending you any warning signs of "burnout"?

- When? _____ Where? _____

- In what situations?

- If so, is there something you could do to decrease your burnout and increase your sense of well-being?

- Do you have a plan? If so, what is it?

EXERCISE 6. YOUR LIFETIME DRAMA

Find a quiet place where you can sit down and not be interrrupted. With your eyes closed, project your life drama onto an imaginary screen. Watch it from its beginning up to the present moment. Take your time. After your experience, consider:

- Is your life drama a comedy, a farce, a saga, a soap opera, a melodrama, a tragedy, or what?

- Does your play have a script theme? If so, is it success-oriented or failure-oriented? Constructive, destructive, or nonproductive?

- How do you see yourself structuring time in various scenes and acts?

- Imagine an audience watching your play. Do they applaud, cry, boo, laugh, go to sleep, want their money back, or what?

- Now, ask yourself, "Was I ever told how I would end up?" If so, are you living up to this expectation? How do you think people like yourself actually do end up?

  How does your life drama—your script—influence your health and work?

- Does it produce distress and burnout?

- If so, how do your experience it emotionally? Physically?

- How does it affect your performance?

  Looking at your life from this persepective, do you see ways you want to structure your life's time differently?

- On the job?

- Off the job?

EXERCISE 7. YOUR ORGANIZATION DRAMA

If you projected what goes on in your organization on a movie screen, what would it look like?

- Is it a comedy, tragedy, farce, saga, or what?

- What continues to happen that is good for everyone?

- What happens that interferes with cooperation, job satisfaction, and improved working conditions?

- What happens that interferes with or blocks the patients' best interests?

- What happens that is bad for your health?

- What changes would improve the situation for the patients, various staff members, and you?

- Which of these changes are possible?

PEOPLE CAN MAKE CONTRACTS FOR CHANGE

Making contracts is part of everyone's daily life. People sign work contracts with employers to change their salaries; they enter marriage contracts with spouses to exchange certain rights and privileges; they sign mortgage contracts with banks, contracts of purchase with department stores, and so on.

Contracts can also be made with others or with oneself around personal change. In order to make contracts, people need to have enough awareness of their approach to life to know what is causing them or others dissatisfaction or undue discomfort. This means getting in touch with their patterns that are not productive and then developing clear ideas and images as to how they want things to be instead. A contract is an Adult commitment to one's self or to someone else to make a change. It needs to be clear, concise, and direct. [10]

Contracts can be fairly easy or difficult, depending on the severity of the problem. They can be short-range goals or can involve lifetime changes. They can be made by one person, two persons, or by a team.

EXERCISE 8. MAKING SHORT-TERM CONTRACTS

Planning to do something and then doing it is a way to learn how to make contracts. Short-term contracts are a very effective way to begin to take charge of your life and your time. By successfully completing small contracts, you will have more confidence and ability to make ones that are more important to you.

To learn this process, select something you could change immediately that would add more meaning to your personal life, such as going to a play or movie you've been wanting to see, going to a new place you're curious about, ringing up an old friend, getting a stylized haircut, etc. Then fill in the form below.

- A short-term personal goal I have that would enhance my life is

- What I need to do about it is

- What I'm willing to do about it is

- I'll know I reached my goal when

- I could sabotage myself by

- If this begins to happen, I can

- When I succeed, I'll celebrate by

EXERCISE 9. A LONG-TERM PERSONAL CONTRACT

Successful completion of major contracts often involves a change in one's script. Even after a firm decision is made, such as losing weight, it may take considerable time to develop new eating and exercising habits so that the weight stays off. As another example, a decision to upgrade professional skills by returning to school may be followed by months, even years, of daily contracting to study.

Now practice how to make a long-term contract.

- A long-term goal I want to achieve that would enhance my personal or professional life is

- What I need to do to reach the goal is

- What I'm willing to do is (record each step of your plan) and your potential starting and completion dates for each step.

- I will know when I have achieved each step when

- I might sabotage myself and avoid getting what I want by

- To prevent this from happening, I need to

- If I am not perfect and occasionally "backslide", I could

  instead of

- I will occasionally check out my contract with

- When I have completed this contract, I will celebrate by

EXERCISE 10. CONTRACTING FOR IMPROVED COMMUNICATIONS

Many people would like to improve communications on the job, yet do not explore new options for doing so.

Consider a communication problem in which transactions often cross or carry negative ulterior messages.

- I want improved communications with

  about

- What *I* need to do to achieve this is

- What I'm willing to do is

- Improved communication would show by

- How I might sabotage my goal is

- Therefore, my back-up plan is

Now repeat the exercise, imagining that in spite of the fact that the other person seems unwilling to change, you may be able to improve a communication problem. Let your creative, intuitive Little Professor team up with your Adult.

EXERCISE 11. BUILDING TEAM CONTRACTS

Health care work involves teamwork. Winning teams always use well-planned strategies. Each person on a team may have a different task, yet together their synergy adds up to an organized whole that is greater than any of the parts.

To establish a team contract, work in small groups and discuss these questions:

- What do we want as a *team* that would enhance our work?

- What do we each need to do *personally* to get what we want?

- What do we need to do as a *team* to get what we want?

- What is each of us personally willing to do?

- What are we as a *team* willing to do?

- How will our individual success show?

- And how will our team success show?

- What might we do individually to sabotage our teamwork?

- What might we do as a team to avoid reaching our goal?

- Do we need a back-up plan? _____ If so, what?

- What kind of team celebration is called for?

P.S. FROM THE AUTHORS

We believe that time is precious, that people are important, and that relating to them well enhances the quality of life. We also believe that people do *not* have to be enslaved by their past experiences. They can transcend past influences that are self-defeating and respond more positively in the present. They can activate the Adult ego state in new ways and take more responsibility for their lives. They can appropriately use the nurturing, caring side of the Parent. They can release the life energy and enthusiasm of the Child. By using their total personality in positive, winning ways, people can foster their own health, the health of others, and the health of the organizations in which they work.

NOTES AND REFERENCES

INTRODUCTION

1. Muriel James and Dorothy Jongeward, *Born to Win: Transactional Analysis with Gestalt Experiments* (Reading, Mass.: Addison-Wesley, 1971).

2. Eric Berne, *Games People Play* (New York: Grove Press, 1964).

3. L. James Wylie, Vice President Human Relations & Resources, Lutheran General Hospital, Park Ridge, Illinois.

UNIT 1. THE SCRIPTS PEOPLE LIVE BY

1. Eric Berne, *What Do You Say After You Say Hello?* (New York: Grove Press, 1973), p. 418.

2. Muriel James, *Transactional Analysis for Moms & Dads: What Do You Do with Them Now That You've Got Them?* (Reading, Mass.: Addison-Wesley, 1974).

3. Eric Berne, *Sex in Human Loving* (New York: Simon & Schuster, 1971), p. 193.

4. Fernand Lamaze, *Painless Childbirth: The Lamaze Method* (Chicago: Contemporary Books, 1970); Frederick Leboyer, *Birth Without Violence,* 1st American Edition (New York: Knopf, 1975, (distributed by Random House).

5. For more information on scripts, *see* Dorothy Jongeward and Philip C. Seyer, *Choosing Success: Transactional Analysis on the Job* (New York: Wiley, 1978), pp. 34–36, 175–179.

6. *Also see* James and Jongeward, *Born to Win,* Chapters 4, 7, and 10.

7. Dorothy Jongeward, *Everybody Wins: Transactional Analysis Applied to Organizations,* rev. ed. (Reading, Mass.: Addison-Wesley, 1976).

8. *See* Dorothy Jongeward and Dru Scott, *Women As Winners: Transactional Analysis for Personal Growth* (Reading, Mass.: Addison-Wesley, 1976).

9. For a historical perspective of roles, *see* Muriel James, "The Down Scripting of Women for 115 Generations" in *Techniques in Transactional Analysis: For*

Psychotherapists and Counselors (Reading, Mass.: Addison-Wesley, 1977), pp. 497-506.

10. For information on the changing laws and roles regarding working women, *see* Dorothy Jongeward and Dru Scott, *Affirmative Action for Women: A Practical Guide for Women and Management* (Reading, Mass.: Addison-Wesley, 1976).

11. Eric Berne, *Principles of Group Treatment* (New York: Oxford University Press, 1964), pp. 269-278.

12. Eric Berne, "Standard Nomenclature, Transactional Nomenclature," *"Transactional Analysis Bulletin* **8**, 32 (October 1979): 112.

13. Muriel James, *The OK Boss* (Reading, Mass.: Addison-Wesley, 1975), pp. 55-62.

14. *Also see* Jongeward and Seyer, *Choosing Success*, pp. 30-34.

UNIT 2. PERSONALITIES PEOPLE DEVELOP

1. Berne, *Principles of Group Treatment*, p. 364.

2. Eric Berne, *Transactional Analysis in Psychotherapy* (New York: Grove Press, 1961), p. 32.

3. James and Jongeward, *Born to Win*, p. 102.

4. "Natural Medicine" (West Nyack, N.Y.: Parker, May 29, 1979), p. 4.

5. Muriel James and Louis Savary, *A New Self* (Reading, Mass.: Addison-Wesley, 1977).

6. Berne, *Transactional Analysis in Psychotherapy*, p. 51.

7. Berne, *Transactional Analysis in Psychotherapy*, p. 62.

UNIT 3. THE TRANSACTIONS PEOPLE USE

1. For situations in which crossed and ulterior transactions are sometimes appropriate, *see* James, *The OK Boss,* pp. 92-100. For a TA tape on *The OK*

Boss and a focus on management styles, contact Success Motivation Institute, 5000 Lakewood Drive, Waco, Texas 76710. For information on a tape by Muriel James, "Changing Yourself Through Transactional Analysis," write to Psychology Today Cassettes, Dept. A 1080, P.O. Box 278, Pratt Station, Brooklyn, New York 11205.

2. Claude M. Steiner, *Games Alcoholics Play: The Analysis of Life Scripts* (New York: Grove Press, 1971).

UNIT 4. STROKES AND PSYCHOLOGICAL TRADING STAMPS

1. Berne, *Games People Play*, p. 15.

2. Eric Berne, *The Structure and Dynamics of Organizations and Groups* (Philadelphia: Lippincott, 1963), p. 157.

3. Second Chance, American Medical Association Rental Film Library, c/o Association Films, 866 3rd Avenue, New York, N.Y. 10022.

4. James and Jongeward, *Born to Win*, pp. 45-46.

5. For more in-depth information on strokes as units of motivation on the job, *see* Jongeward and Seyer, *Choosing Success*, and Jongeward, *Everybody Wins.*

6. For information about Management Contact, a multimedia TA training program for managers featuring Dorothy Jongeward, contact Deltak, Inc., 220 Kensington Road, Oak Brook, Illinois 60521.

7. Dolores Kreiger, "Therapeutic Touch: The Imprimatur of Nursing," *American Journal of Nursing* 75, 5 (May 1975): 784-787.

8. The term "target stroking" was designed by Muriel James and refers to specific strokes for each ego state. For theory and application to management, *see* James, *The OK Boss*, pp. 72-89.

9. For further information contrasting strokes for women and men, *see* Jongeward and Scott, *Women As Winners,* and Jongeward and Scott, *Affirmative Action for Women and Management.*

10. Berne, *Principles of Group Treatment*, pp. 286-288.

11. The phrases "warm fuzzy" and "cold prickly" were first introduced by Claude Steiner in his story *Warm Fuzzy Tale* (Sacramento, Calif.: Jalmar Press, 1977).

UNIT 5. GAMES PEOPLE PLAY

1. *See* Stephen B. Karpman, "Fairy Tales and Script Drama Analysis," *Transactional Analysis Bulletin* 7, 26 (April 1968): 39-43.

2. Berne, *Games People Play. See also* Berne, *What Do You Say After You Say Hello*, pp. 23-25, 156-158, 417.

3. For an in-depth discussion of games played in organizations, *see* Jongeward, *Everybody Wins,* Chapters 2 and 3. Many games are covered in the cassette "Everybody Wins" (Success Motivation Institute, Waco, Texas) and the cassette "The OK Boss" (Success Motivation Institute, Waco, Texas). *Also see* Jongeward and Seyer, *Choosing Success*, Chapters 6 and 7.

4. Karpman, "Fairy Tales."

5. John James, "The Game Plan," *Transactional Analysis Journal* 3, 4 (October 1973): 14-17. *See also* Muriel James and Dorothy Jongeward, *The People Book: Transactional Analysis for Students* (Reading, Mass.: Addison-Wesley, 1975), Chapters 18-22; and James, *Techniques in Transactional Analysis*, p. 73.

6. *See also* Pamela Levin and Eric Berne, "Games Nurses Play," *American Journal of Nursing* (March 1972).

UNIT 6. EGO STATE BLOCKS TO PROBLEM SOLVING

1. James, *Techniques in Psychotherapy,* p. 76.

2. James and Jongeward, *Born to Win*, p. 234.

3. *Honolulu Star Bulletin*, December 14, 1978.

4. *See* Muriel James, "Pastoral Counseling," in Eric Berne, *A Layman's Guide to Psychiatry & Psychoanalysis,* 3rd ed. (New York: Simon and Schuster, 1968), pp. 313-316. *See also* Muriel James, "The Use of Structural Analysis in Pastoral Counseling," in James, *Techniques in Transactional Analysis,* pp. 505-517.

5. *Oakland Tribune*, Oakland, Calif., September 30, 1978.

6. Berne, *Transactional Analysis in Psychotherapy*, p. 62.

7. Berne, *Principles of Group Treatment*, p. 311.

UNIT 7. TIME STRUCTURING AND CONTRACTING FOR CHANGE

1. Jongeward and Seyer, *Choosing Success*, pp. 170-171.

2. Jongeward and Seyer, *Choosing Success,* p. 177.

3. *See* Taibi Kahler with Hedges Capers, "The Miniscript," *Transactional Analysis Journal* 4, 1 (January 1974): 26-41.

4. Hans Selye, *Stress Without Distress* (Philadelphia: Lippincott, 1974), p. 147; *see also* Kenneth R. Pelletier, *Mind As Healer, Mind As Slayer* (New York: Dell, 1979).

5. James and Savary, *A New Self,* pp. 299-302.

6. Herbert Benson, *The Relaxation Response* (New York: Morrow, 1975).

7. Side A: "Deep Relaxation Exercise" and Side B: "Concentration & Awareness Exercises," a cassette tape narrated by Dorothy Jongeward and designed for relaxation. For information, write to Transactional Analysis Management Institute, Inc., 724 Ironbark Court, Orinda, California 94563.

8. Muriel James, "Laugh Therapy: Theory, Procedures, Results in Clinical and Special Fields," *Transactional Analysis Journal* 9, 4 (October 1979): 244-250; *see also* Norman Cousins, "Anatomy of an Illness (As Perceived by the Patient)," *New England Journal of Medicine* 295 (December 23, 1976): 1458-1463.

9. Rosalind Forbes, "Job Stress and Personality," *Western's World* (Beverly Hills, Calif.: Frank M. Hiteshaw & Associates, September/October 1979), pp. 40-43, 64-67, 71.

10. For a detailed procedure for establishing both individual and interpersonal contracts, *see* James and Savary, *A New Self*, pp. 83-105, 195-209. For a focus on how to develop effective and efficient contracts on the job, *see* James, *The OK Boss,* pp. 148-162.

APPENDIX A
BOOKS AND MATERIALS

We have collaborated on these transactional analysis books:

- *Born to Win: Transactional Analysis with Gestalt Experiments* (Reading, Mass.: Addison-Wesley, 1971).

- *Winning with People: Group Exercises in Transactional Analysis* (Reading, Mass.: Addison-Wesley, 1973).

- *The People Book: Transactional Analysis for Students* (Reading, Mass.: Addison-Wesley, 1975).

Also available are a cassette tape of *Born to Win*, produced by Success Motivation Institute, Waco, Texas, and a slide-tape production on winners and losers: "On Being Yourself" (Reading, Mass.: Addison-Wesley).

These are our works that have to do directly with management and interpersonal effectiveness on the job:

- Muriel James, *The OK Boss* (Reading, Mass.: Addison-Wesley, 1975).

- Dorothy Jongeward and Contributors, *Everybody Wins: Transactional Analysis Applied to Organizations* (Reading, Mass.: Addison-Wesley, revised 1976).

- Dorothy Jongeward and Dru Scott, *Affirmative Action for Women: A Practical Guide for Women and Management* (Reading, Mass.: Addison-Wesley, revised 1975).

- Dorothy Jongeward and Philip Seyer, *Choosing Success: Transactional Analysis on the Job* (New York: Wiley, 1978).

Our other books and learning tools include:

Books

Muriel James, *Born to Love: Transactional Analysis in the Church* (Reading, Mass.: Addison-Wesley, 1973).

———— , *Marriage Is for Loving* (Reading, Mass.: Addison-Wesley, 1979).

———— , *Transactional Analysis For Moms and Dads: What Do You Do with Them Now That You've Got Them?* (Reading, Mass.: Addison-Wesley, 1974).

Muriel James and Louis Savary, *The Power at the Bottom of the Well: TA with a Biblical Perspective* (New York: Harper & Row, 1974).

———— , *The Heart of Friendship* (New York: Harper & Row, 1976).

———— , *A New Self: Self Therapy with TA* (Reading, Mass.: Addison-Wesley, 1977).

Muriel James and Contributors, *Techniques in TA: For Psychotherapists and Counselors* (Reading, Mass.: Addison-Wesley, 1977).

Dorothy Jongeward and Dru Scott, *Women As Winners: Transactional Analysis for Personal Growth* (Reading, Mass.: Addison-Wesley, 1976).

Cassettes

"The OK Boss," by Muriel James, focusing on management styles, produced by Success Motivation Institute, 5000 Lakewood Drive, Waco, Texas.

"Changing Yourself Through Transactional Analysis" (an interview with Muriel James), produced by Psychology Today Cassettes, Dept. A 1080, P.O. Box 278, Pratt Station, Brooklyn, New York 11205.

"Everybody Wins," produced by Success Motivation Institute, Waco, Texas. Side A: "Deep Relaxation Exercise" and Side B: "Concentration and Awareness Exercises," narrated by Dorothy Jongeward. For information, contact Transactional Analysis Management Institute, Inc., 724 Ironbark Court, Orinda, California 94563.

"Transactional Analysis Overview Cassette Program," narrated by Dorothy Jongeward. For information, contact Transactional Analysis Management Institute, 724 Ironbark Court, Orinda, California 94563.

Learning Programs

Management Contact, a multimedia training program featuring Dorothy Jongeward, produced by Deltak, Inc., 220 Kensington Road, Oak Brook, Illinois 60521.

For your information, these are Dr. Eric Berne's major books:

Games People Play (New York: Grove Press, 1964).

Layman's Guide to Psychiatry and Psychoanalysis (New York: Simon & Schuster, 1957).

Principles of Group Treatment (New York: Oxford University Press, 1964).

Sex in Human Loving (New York: Simon & Schuster, 1971).

The Structure and Dynamics of Organizations and Groups (Philadelphia: Lippincott, 1963).

Transactional Analysis in Psychotherapy (New York: Grove Press, 1961).

What Do You Say After You Say Hello? (New York: Grove Press, 1972).

For information about training in transactional analysis, other books, and membership in the professional organization, write to:

International Transactional Analysis Association
1772 Vallejo Street
San Francisco, California 94123
Telephone number: (415) 885-5992

APPENDIX B
POSSIBLE EGO STATE RESPONSES

ANALYZING EGO STATE VOCABULARY AND BODY LANGUAGE

Parent

Sample Words and Phrases

should, don't, must, ought, always, never, now what, if I were you, let me help you, because I said so, don't ask questions, do not disturb, be good, what will the neighbors say, there there, sweetie, honey, and dearie.

You are: bad, good, stupid, ugly, beautiful, smart, ridiculous, naughty, evil, talented, cute, all wet, horrible, a trial, a blessing, a brat, an angel, absurd, asinine, shocking.

Try, don't be afraid; come on now; see, it doesn't hurt; don't worry; I'll take care of you; here's something to make you feel better.

Gestures and Postures

Pointing an accusing or threatening finger; a pat on the back; consoling touch; pounding on the table; rolling eyes upward in disgust; tapping feet or wringing hands in impatience; shaking head to imply "no-no" or "OK!" Arms folded across chest with chin set; face tilted up looking down nose; holding and/or rocking someone.

Tone of Voice

Sneering, punitive, condescending, encouraging, supportive, sympathetic.

Facial Expressions

Scowl; encouraging nod; furrowed brow; set jaw; angry; sympathetic or proud eyes; smile; frown; loving; hostile; disapproving.

Adult

Sample Words and Phrases

How; when; who; what; where; why; probability; alternative; result; yes; no; what are the facts; this is not proven but opinion; check it out; what has been done to correct it so far; it's 4:30 P.M.; what are the reasons; have you tried this; mix two parts with one part; this is how it works; let's take it apart and look at it; let's look for the causes; according to the statistics . . . ; change is indicated; the meeting is at 2:00 P.M. Friday.

Gestures and Postures

Straight (not stiff) posture; eye contact that's level; pointing something out (i.e., direction) with finger; listening by giving feedback and checking out understanding; interested.

Tone of Voice

Clear without undue emotion; calm; straight; confident; inquiring and giving information.

Facial Expressions

Thoughtful; watching attentively; quizzical; lively; here-and-now responsiveness; eyes alert, confident.

Child

Sample Words and Phrases

Gosh, wow; gee whiz; can't; won't; gimme; dunno; want; wish; (any kind of baby talk); mine; eek. Ain't I cute; look at me now; did I do all right; I'm scared; help me; do it for me; nobody loves me; you make me cry; it's your fault; I didn't do it; he's no good; mine is better than yours; I'm going to tell on you; you'll be sorry; I wanta go home; let's play; phooey on this old job; more candy; I hope everybody loves me.

Gestures and Postures

Slumped; dejected; temper tantrums; batting eyelashes; joyful or exhilarated posture; curling up; skipping; squirming; nose thumbing; (other obscene gestures); nail biting; raising hand to speak.

Tone of Voice

Giggling; gurgling; whining; manipulating; sweet talk; asking permission; swearing; spitefulness; teasing; sullen silence; taunting; needling; belly laughing; excitement; talking fast and loud; playfulness.

Facial Expression

Teary eyed; pouting; eyes looking upward at another; downcast eyes; joyfulness; excited; curious; psyching things out; tilted head; flirty; looking innocent and wide-eyed; woebegone; helplessness; admiration.

APPENDIX C
STRESS QUIZ EVALUATION

If your score is between 134 and 150, you possess personality characteristics that are likely to generate a great deal of stress for you on the job. Your personality causes you to create much of your own stress, and this may limit your ability to function well under pressure.

A score between 114 and 135 indicates that there is room for improvement. This person is usually unable to handle high amounts of stress for prolonged periods of time.

There is a good balance between 74 and 115. You will have to make a conscious effort, however, to keep your behavior on the positive end of the scale when going through stressful situations.

If your score is between 44 and 75, it is not likely that your personality aggravates your reaction to stress. You probably are an individual who feels able to handle and control most situations.

A score between 30 and 45 indicates that you possess characteristics that defuse much of the stress in your life. Your qualities make you a candidate for a leadership position, since you function well under pressure.